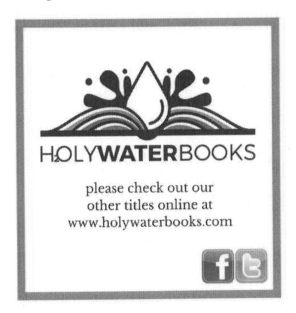

please check out our
other titles online at
www.holywaterbooks.com

Cover design by Scott L. Smith

SAVE THE DATE!

Next year's Men of the Immaculata Conference
is currently scheduled for
February 29, 2020

VISIT

www.MenoftheImmaculata.com

for date updates,
to register starting mid-year, and
to subscribe to our mailing list for discounts and announce-
ments

THE MEN OF THE IMMACULATA

present

Catholic Men's Conference 2019

and the

THE CATHOLIC MANBOOK

A CALL
TO BATTLE:
CONSECRATION

CATHOLIC
MEN'S
CONFERENCE

ST. GEORGE, BATON ROUGE, LA · 3/9/19

A SPECIAL THANK YOU
TO OUR HOSTS
St. George Parish and
St. George Men's Club

TABLE OF CONTENTS

I.
SPEAKERS NOTES

FATHER DONALD CALLOWAY, MIC

Biography

Fr. Calloway, a convert to Catholicism, is a member of the Congregation of Marian Fathers of the Immaculate Conception. Before his conversion to Catholicism, he was a high school dropout who had been kicked out of a foreign country, institutionalized twice, and thrown in jail multiple times. He is the author of 7 books including *No Turning Back* and *Champions of the Rosary*.

Notes Section

_____
_____
_____
_____
_____
_____
_____
_____
_____
_____
_____
_____
_____
_____
_____
_____
_____
_____
_____
_____
_____
_____
_____
_____
_____
_____
_____
_____
_____

TIM STAPLES

Biography

Tim returned to Christ through the witness of televangelists, and after serving with the Marines attended Jimmy Swaggart Bible College, determined to prove Catholicism wrong. However, he studied his way into a Catholic conversion in 1988. Tim has been working in Catholic apologetics since 1994, and is the Director of Apologetics and Evangelization at Catholic Answers.

Notes Section

_____

_____

_____

_____

_____

_____

_____

_____

_____

_____

_____

_____

_____

_____

_____

_____

_____

_____

_____

_____

_____

_____

_____

_____

_____

_____

_____

MEN OF THE IMMACULATA

SISTER TRACEY MATTHIA DUGAS

Biography

Sr. Tracey Matthia Dugas is a Cajun girl from St. Martin-ville, Louisiana. As a teen, one of her big goals in life was to get a job at the mall so she could "get a really good discount at The Gap." Yet at the same time she hungered for something more and kept asking herself, "What do I really want?"

Her favorite thing about being consecrated to God is that she's God's "audio-visual," called to communicate him and his love and truth to everyone.

"I'm always amazed at how God can speak to the heart through music! I pray that he will speak to you of his immense love and never-failing mercy."

CHEF JOHN FOLSE

Biography

Chef John Folse, born in St. James Parish in 1946, learned early that the secrets of Cajun cooking lay in the unique ingredients of Louisiana's swamp floor pantry. Folse seasoned these raw ingredients with his passion for Louisiana culture and cuisine, and from his cast iron pots emerged Chef John Folse & Company.

When Folse opened Lafitte's Landing Restaurant in 1978 in Donaldsonville, he set out to market his restaurant by taking "a taste of Louisiana" worldwide. He introduced Louisiana's indigenous cuisine to Japan in 1985, Beijing in 1986 and Hong Kong and Paris in 1987.

In 1988, Folse made international headlines with the opening of "Lafitte's Landing East" in Moscow during the Presidential Summit between Ronald Reagan and Mikhail Gorbachev.

In 1989, Folse was the first non-Italian chef to create the Vatican State Dinner in Rome. The previous year, the Louisiana Legislature gave him the title of "Louisiana's Culinary Ambassador to the World."

The international success of Folse's cornerstone property, Lafitte's Landing Restaurant, spawned the incorporation of several other Chef John Folse & Company properties. White Oak Plantation in 1986 established Folse's catering and events management division. Chef John Folse & Company Publishing, since 1989, has produced nine cookbooks in his Cajun and Creole series, plus a novel, two children's books and a religious memoir by other authors.

"A Taste of Louisiana" is Folse's international television series produced by Louisiana Public Broadcasting since 1990.

Chef John Folse & Company Manufacturing, since 1991, is one of the few chef-owned food manufacturing companies in America producing custom-manufactured foods for restaurants as well as retail and foodservice industries. In January 2005 a new USDA manufacturing plant opened in Donaldsonville, and in 2007 growing demands pushed the plant to expand. In 2008, Folse cut the ribbon of his expanded 68,000 square-foot food manufacturing plant.

More than thirty years of culinary excellence later, Folse is still adding ingredients to the corporate gumbo he calls Chef John Folse & Company, which is as diverse as the Louisiana landscape, and he would not want it any other way.

For more on Chef John Folse, visit www.jfolse.com.

Notes Section

_____
_____
_____
_____
_____
_____
_____
_____
_____
_____
_____
_____
_____
_____
_____
_____
_____
_____
_____
_____
_____
_____
_____
_____
_____
_____
_____
_____
_____
_____

II.
THE ROSARY

How to Pray the Rosary

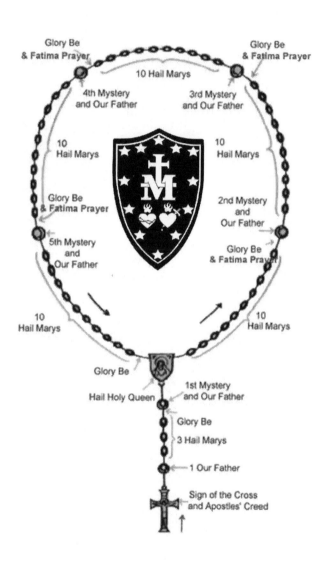

Prayers Recited with Rosary

The "Apostles' Creed"
I believe in God, the Father Almighty, Creator of heaven and earth; and in Jesus Christ, His only Son, our Lord; Who was conceived by the Holy Spirit, born of the Virgin Mary, suffered under Pontius Pilate, was crucified, died, and was buried. He descended into hell; the third day He arose again from the dead. He ascended into heaven, and sits at the right hand of God, the Father Almighty; from thence He shall come to judge the living and the dead. **I believe in the Holy Spirit, the Holy Catholic Church, the communion of Saints, the forgiveness of sins, the resurrection of the body and life everlasting. Amen.**

Announce the Mystery before beginning the "Our Father (see next section):

The "Our Father"
Our Father, Who art in heaven, hallowed be Thy name; Thy kingdom come; Thy will be done on earth as it is in heaven.
**Give us this day our daily bread;
and forgive us our trespasses
as we forgive those who trespass against us;
and lead us not into temptation,
but deliver us from evil. Amen.**

The "Hail Mary"
Hail Mary, full of grace, the Lord is with thee; blessed art thou among women, and blessed is the fruit of thy womb, Jesus. **Holy Mary, Mother of God, pray for us sinners, now and at the hour of our death. Amen.**

The "Glory Be"
Glory be to the Father,
and to the Son,
and to the Holy Spirit,
as it was in the beginning,
is now, and ever shall be,
world without end. Amen.

After each Decade (following the "Glory Be"):

The Prayer Requested by the Blessed Virgin Mary at Fatima
O my Jesus, forgive us our sins, save us from the fires of hell,
lead all souls to Heaven, especially those who have most
need of your mercy.

After the Rosary:

The "Hail, Holy Queen" (Or *Salve Regina*)
HAIL, HOLY QUEEN, Mother of Mercy, our life, our sweetness and our hope! To thee do we cry, poor banished children of Eve; to thee do we send up our sighs, mourning and
weeping in this vale of tears. Turn then, most gracious advocate, thine eyes of mercy toward us, and after this our exile,
show unto us the blessed fruit of thy womb, Jesus. O clem-
ent, O loving, O sweet Virgin Mary!

> V. Pray for us, O Holy Mother of God.
> R. That we may be made worthy of the promises of
> Christ.

Let us pray. O GOD, whose only begotten Son, by His life,
death, and resurrection, has purchased for us the rewards of
eternal life, grant, we beseech Thee, that meditating upon
these mysteries of the Most Holy Rosary of the Blessed Vir-

gin Mary, we may imitate what they contain and obtain what they promise, through the same Christ Our Lord. Amen.

Prayer to St. Joseph (optional)

Introduction
This prayer to Saint Joseph—spouse of the Virgin Mary, foster father of Jesus, and patron saint of the universal Church—was composed by Pope Leo XIII in his 1889 encyclical, *Quamquam Pluries.* . . . He asked that it be added to the end of the Rosary, especially during the month of October, which is dedicated to the Rosary. The prayer is enriched with a partial indulgence (*Handbook of Indulgences*, conc. 19), and may be said after the customary *Salve Regina* ("Hail, Holy Queen") and concluding prayer. It may also be used to conclude other Marian devotions.

Prayer
To you, O blessed Joseph,
do we come in our tribulation,
and having implored the help of your most holy Spouse,
we confidently invoke your patronage also.

Through that charity which bound you
to the Immaculate Virgin Mother of God
and through the paternal love
with which you embraced the Child Jesus,
we humbly beg you graciously to regard the inheritance
which Jesus Christ has purchased by his Blood,
and with your power and strength to aid us in our necessities.
O most watchful guardian of the Holy Family,
defend the chosen children of Jesus Christ;
O most loving father, ward off from us

every contagion of error and corrupting influence;
O our most mighty protector, be kind to us
and from heaven assist us in our struggle
with the power of darkness.

As once you rescued the Child Jesus from deadly peril,
so now protect God's Holy Church
from the snares of the enemy and from all adversity;
shield, too, each one of us by your constant protection,
so that, supported by your example and your aid,
we may be able to live piously, to die in holiness,
and to obtain eternal happiness in heaven.
Amen.

MYSTERIES OF THE ROSARY

As suggested by the Pope St. John Paul the Great,
the Joyful mysteries are said on Monday and Saturday,
the Luminous on Thursday, the Sorrowful on Tuesday and
Friday, and the Glorious on Wednesday and Sunday (with
this exception: Sundays of Christmas season - The Joyful;
Sundays of Lent - Sorrowful). See below for the full listing of
the different sets of mysteries.

Joyful Mysteries	Monday	Saturday
Sorrowful	Tuesday	Friday
Glorious	Wednesday	Sunday
Luminous	Thursday	

The **Five Joyful Mysteries** are traditionally prayed on the
Mondays, Saturdays, and Sundays of Advent:
1. The Annunciation
2. The Visitation
3. The Nativity

4. The Presentation in the Temple
5. The Finding in the Temple

The **Five Sorrowful Mysteries** are traditionally prayed on the Tuesdays, Fridays, and Sundays of Lent:
1. The Agony in the Garden
2. The Scourging at the Pillar
3. The Crowning with Thorns
4. The Carrying of the Cross
5. The Crucifixion and Death

The **Five Glorious Mysteries** are traditionally prayed on the Wednesday and Sundays outside of Lent and Advent:
1. The Resurrection
2. The Ascension
3. The Descent of the Holy Spirit
4. The Assumption
5. The Coronation of Mary

The **Five Luminous Mysteries** are traditionally prayed on Thursdays:
1. The Baptism of Christ in the Jordan
2. The Wedding Feast at Cana
3. Jesus' Proclamation of the Coming of the Kingdom of God
4. The Transfiguration
5. The Institution of the Eucharist

ROSARY PRAYERS IN SPANISH

Sign of the Cross	En el nombre del Padre, y del Hijo, y del Espíritu Santo. Amen.
Apostles Creed	Creo en Dios, Padre todopoderoso, creador del Cielo y de la Tierra. Creo en

Jesucristo su único Hijo, Nuestro Señor, que fue concebido por obra y gracia del Espíritu Santo; nació de Santa María Virgen; padeció bajo el poder de Poncio Pilato; fue crucificado, muerto y sepultado; descendió a los infiernos; al tercer día resucitó de entre los muertos; subió a los cielos y está a la diestra de Dios Padre; desde allí ha de venir a juzgar a los vivos y a los muertos. Creo en el Espíritu Santo, en la Santa Iglesia Católica, la comumión de los Santos en el perdon de los pecados la resurrección de los muertos y la vida eterna. Amen.

Our Father

Padre nuestro, que estás en el cielo. Santificado sea tu nombre. Venga tu reino. Hágase tu voluntad en la tierra como en el cielo. Danos hoy nuestro pan de cada día. Perdona nuestras ofensas, como también nosotros perdonamos a los que nos ofenden. No nos dejes caer en tentación y líbranos del mal. Amen.

Hail Mary

Dios te salve, María. Llena eres de gracia: El Señor es contigo. Bendita tú eres entre todas las mujeres. Y bendito es el fruto de tu vientre: Jesús. Santa María, Madre de Dios, ruega por nosotros pecadores, ahora y en la hora de nuestra muerte. Amen.

Glory Be

Gloria al Padre, al Hijo y al Espíritu Santo. Como era en el principio, ahora y siempre, por los siglos de los siglos.

Amen.

Oh My Jesus

Oh mi Jesús, perdónanos nuestros pecados, líbranos del fuego del infierno, lleva todas las almas al cielo, especialmente las mas necesitadas de tu misericordia. Amen.

Hail Holy Queen

Dios te salve, Reina y Madre de misericordia, vida, dulzura y esperanza nuestra, Dios te salve. A ti clamamos los desterrados hijos de Eva. A ti suspiramos gimiendo y llorando en este valle de lágrimas. Ea, pues, Señora, abogada nuestra: vuelve a nosotros esos tus ojos misericordiosos. Y después de este destierro, muéstranos a Jesús, fruto bendito de tu vientre. Oh clemente, oh piadosa, oh dulce Virgen María. Ruega por nosotros, Santa Madre de Dios, para que seamos dignos de las promesas de Cristo. Amen.

Final Prayer

Oh Dios de quién Único Hijo nos ha otorgado los beneficios de la vida eterna, concédenos la gracia que te pedimos mientras meditamos los Misterios del Mas Santo Rosario de la Bienaventurada Virgen María, debemos imitar lo que contienen y obtener lo que prometen, a través del mismo Cristo Nuestro Señor. Amen.

THE ROSARY FOR LIFE

The Rosary for Life is recited in the same manner as the traditional rosary, except that each mystery includes a special meditation on the dignity of human life. This version was written by Father Frank Pavone of Priests for Life. Another version is available from the United States Conference of Catholic Bishops.

The Glorious Mysteries

The Resurrection
Christ is Risen! By his Resurrection, He has destroyed the power of death, and therefore the power of abortion. The outcome of the battle for Life has already been decided: Life is victorious! Let us pray that all prolifers will spread this victory to every segment of our society.

The Ascension
By ascending to the Father's throne, Christ takes our human nature, given to us in the womb, to the heights of heaven. He shows us that human beings are made to be raised to heaven, not thrown in the garbage. Let us pray that the world may learn this truth and reject abortion.

The Descent of the Holy Spirit
The Holy Spirit is the Advocate: He pleads our cause, for we cannot save ourselves. We pray that He will make us advocates for the babies, who cannot speak or write or vote or protest or even pray.

The Assumption
The Blessed Virgin Mary was taken body and soul into heaven because she is the Mother of God. Mother and child are

united. The Assumption reminds us that they belong together. We pray that society will see that it cannot love women while killing their children, and cannot save children without helping their mothers. We pray that people will be touched by the pro-life question, "Why can't we love them both?"

The Coronation
Mary is the Queen of the Universe. The Church teaches that she is the greatest creature, second only to God Himself. The Church defends the dignity of women. We pray that people will understand that to be pro-life means to be pro-woman, and that to be pro-woman demands that we be pro-life.

The Joyful Mysteries

The Annunciation
Mary is troubled by the angel's greeting, yet rejoices to do God's will. Let us pray that those who are troubled by their pregnancy may have the grace to trust in God's will.

The Visitation
John the Baptist leapt for joy in his mother's womb. We pray that people may realize that abortion is not about children who "might" come into the world, but is about children who are already in the world, living and growing in the womb, and are scheduled to be killed.

The Nativity
God Himself was born as a child. The greatness of a person does not depend on size, for the newborn King is very small. Let us pray for an end to prejudice against the tiny babies threatened by abortion.

The Presentation

The Child is presented in the Temple because the Child belongs to God. Children are not the property of their parents, nor of the government. They, and we, belong to God Himself.

The Finding of Jesus in the Temple

The boy Jesus was filled with wisdom, because He is God. Let us pray that all people may see the wisdom of His teachings about the dignity of life, and may understand that this teaching is not an opinion, but the truth.

The Sorrowful Mysteries

The Agony in the Garden

Let us pray for mothers and fathers who are in agony because they are tempted to abort a child. May they be given the good news that there are alternatives, and may they make use of the help that is available.

The Scourging

As Christ's flesh was torn by the instruments of those who scourged Him, so the bodies of babies in the womb are torn by the instruments of the abortionists. Let us pray that abortionists may repent of these acts of child-killing.

The Crowning With Thorns

Jesus suffered the pain of thorns in His head, and did so silently. We pray for the mothers and fathers of aborted children. So many of them suffer deep grief and regret over a choice they can never reverse. So many suffer in silence, because others tell them it's no big deal.

The Carrying of the Cross
Jesus was not condemned by the power of wicked people. He was condemned because of the silence of good people. Silence always helps the oppressor, never the victim. Let us pray that we may never be silent about abortion, but rather will clearly speak up to save babies from death.

The Crucifixion
As we ponder the death of Christ, let us remember the many women who have died from so-called "safe, legal" abortions. Let us ask forgiveness and mercy for them. May their memory save other women from making this tragic mistake.

The Luminous Mysteries

Christ is Baptized in the Jordan
When Jesus is baptized, the Father's voice is heard: "This is my beloved Son." All are called to become adopted sons and daughters of God through baptism. We pray that children in the womb may be protected, so that they may be born and welcomed into the Christian community by baptism.

Christ is made known at the Wedding of Cana
Jesus revealed His glory by the miracle at Cana. The new couple was blessed not only with wine, but with faith in Christ. Let us pray for strong marriages, rooted in the Lord, and open to the gift of new life.

Christ proclaims the Kingdom and Calls All to Conversion
"Repent and believe the Good News." Let us pray that these first words of Jesus' public ministry may be heard by all who have committed abortion. May they know that the Lord calls them to conversion, and may they experience life-giving repentance.

The Transfiguration
Christ is transformed on the mountain, and the disciples see His glory. May the eyes of all people be transformed, that they may see each and every human life as a reflection of the glory of God Himself.

Jesus gives us the Eucharist
"This is My Body, given up for you." The Eucharist teaches us how to live and how to love. Let us pray that parents who sacrifice the babies for the sake of themselves may learn instead to put themselves aside for the sake of their babies.

Our Lady's 15 Promises for Praying the Rosary

[The following is adapted and excerpted from *Return to Christ* by Dominick Pepito, Catholic Life International]

Besides the Indulgences attached to the Rosary discussed in *The Secret of the Rosary*, which is included in this book, Our Lady revealed to St. Dominic and Blessed Alan de la Roche additional benefits for those who devoutly pray the Rosary. Our Lady's promises are shown below in in bold. Additional explanations are provided below each promise. Note that the Rosary is the prayer (non-Liturgical) with the most published Magisterial and Papal documents expounding on its excellence. Vatican II's summary on Our Lady is contained in *Lumen Gentium* chapter VIII.

1. **Whosoever shall faithfully serve me by the recitation of the Rosary shall receive signal graces.**

Signal Graces are those special and unique Graces to help sanctify us in our state in life. See the remaining promises for an explanation for which these will consist. St. Louis de Montfort states emphatically that the best and fastest way to union with Our Lord is via Our Lady [*True Devotion to Mary*, chapter four].

2.   **I promise my special protection and the greatest graces to all those who shall recite the Rosary.**

Our Lady is our Advocate and the channel of all God's Grace to us. Our Lady is simply highlighting that She will watch especially over us who pray the Rosary. (see Lumen Gentium chapter VIII - Our Lady #62) [a great more detail is available on this topic in True Devotion to Mary, chapter four, by St. Louis de Montfort]

3.   **The Rosary shall be a powerful armor against hell, it will destroy vice, decrease sin and defeat heresies.**

This promise, along with the next, is simply the reminder on how fervent prayer will help us all grow in holiness by avoiding sin, especially a prayer with the excellence of the Rosary. An increase in holiness necessarily requires a reduction in sin, vice, and doctrinal errors (heresies). If only the Modernists could be convinced to pray the Rosary! (see *Lumen Gentium* chapter V - The Call to Holiness #42) St. Louis de Montfort states "Since Mary alone crushed all heresies, as we are told by the Church under the guidance of the Holy Spirit (Office of the Blessed Virgin Mary)..." [*True Devotion to Mary* #167]

4.   It will cause good works to flourish; it will obtain for souls the abundant mercy of God; it will withdraw the hearts of men from the love of the world and its vanities, and will lift them to the desire for Eternal Things. Oh, that souls would sanctify themselves by this means.

This promise, along with the previous, is the positive part, that being to live in virtue. Becoming holy is not only avoiding sin, but also growing in virtue. (see *Lumen Gentium* chapter V - The Call to Holiness #42)

5.   **The soul which recommends itself to me by the recitation of the Rosary shall not perish.**

Since Our Lady is our Mother and Advocate, She always assists those who call on Her implicitly by praying the Rosary. The Church reminds us of this in the Memorare prayer, "... never was it known that anyone who fled to your protection, implored your help or sought your intercession, was left unaided ..."

6.   **Whosoever shall recite the Rosary devoutly, applying himself to the consideration of its Sacred Mysteries shall never be conquered by misfortune. God will not chastise him in His justice, he shall not perish by an unprovided death; if he be just he shall remain in the grace of God, and become worthy of Eternal Life.**

This promise highlights the magnitude of Graces that the Rosary brings to whomever prays it. One will draw down

God's Mercy rather than His Justice and will have a final chance to repent (see promise #7). One will not be conquered by misfortune means that Our Lady will obtain for the person sufficient Graces to handle said misfortune (i.e. carry the Crosses allowed by God) without falling into despair. As Sacred Scripture tells us, "For my yoke is sweet and my burden light." (Matthew 11:30)

7. **Whoever shall have a true devotion for the Rosary shall not die without the Sacraments of the Church.**

This promise highlights the benefits of obtaining the most possible Graces at the hour of death via the Sacraments of Confession, Eucharist, and Extreme Unction (Anointing of the Sick). Being properly disposed while receiving these Sacraments near death ensures one's salvation (although perhaps with a detour through Purgatory) since a final repentance is possible.

8. **Those who are faithful to recite the Rosary shall have during their life and at their death the Light of God and the plenitude of His Graces; at the moment of death they shall participate in the Merits of the Saints in Paradise.**

Our Lady highlights the great quantity of Graces obtain through praying the Rosary, which assist us during life and at the moment of death. The merits of the Saints are the gift of God's rewards to those persons who responded to His Grace that they obtained during life, and so Our Lady indicates that She will provide a share of that to us at death.

With this promise and #7 above, Our Lady is providing the means for the person to have a very holy death.

9.   I shall deliver from purgatory those who have been devoted to the Rosary.

Should one require Purgatorial cleansing after death, Our Lady will make a special effort to obtain our release from Purgatory through Her intercession as Advocate.

10.   The faithful children of the Rosary shall merit a high degree of Glory in Heaven.

This promise is a logical consequence of promises #3 and #4 since anyone who truly lives a holier life on earth will obtain a higher place in Heaven. The closer one is to God while living on earth, the close that person is to Him also in Heaven. The Catechism of the Catholic Church states "Spiritual progress tends toward ever more union with Christ." (*Catechism of the Catholic Church*, paragraph 2014)

11.   You shall obtain all you ask of me by recitation of the Rosary.

This promise emphasizes Our Lady's role as our Advocate and Mediatrix of all Graces. Of course, all requests are subject to God's Most Perfect Will. God will always grant our request if it is beneficial for our soul, and Our Lady will only intercede for us when our request is good for our salvation. (see *Lumen Gentium* chapter VIII - Our Lady #62)

12.   All those who propagate the Holy Rosary shall be aided by me in their necessities.

If one promotes the praying of the Rosary, Our Lady emphasizes Her Maternal care for us by obtaining many Graces (i.e.
spiritual necessities) and also material necessities (neither
excess nor luxury), all subject to the Will of God of course.

13.   **I have obtained from my Divine Son that all
      the advocates of the Rosary shall have for in-
      tercessors the entire Celestial Court during
      their life and at the hour of death.**

Since Our Lady is our Advocate, She brings us additional
assistance during our life and at our death from all the saints
in Heaven (the Communion of Saints). See paragraphs 954
through 959 in the *Catechism of the Catholic Church*.

14.   **All who recite the Rosary are my Sons, and
      brothers of my Only Son Jesus Christ.**

Since the Rosary is a most excellent prayer focused on Jesus
and His Life and activities in salvation history, it brings us
closer to Our Lord and Our Lady. Doctrinally, Our Lady is
our Mother and Jesus is our Eldest Brother, besides being
our God. (see *Lumen Gentium* chapter VIII - Our Lady #62)

15.   **Devotion to my Rosary is a great sign of pre-
      destination.**

Predestination in this context means that, by the sign which
is present to a person from the action of devoutly praying
the Rosary, God has pre-ordained your salvation. Absolute
certainty of salvation can only be truly known if God reveals
it to a person because, although we are given sufficient Grace
during life, our salvation depends upon our response to said
Grace. (See *Summa Theologica*, Question 23 for a detailed

theological explanation). Said another way, if God has guaranteed a person's salvation but has not revealed it to Him, God would want that person to pray the Rosary because of all the benefits and Graces obtained. Therefore the person gets a hint by devotion to the Rosary. This is not to say that praying the Rosary guarantees salvation - by no means. In looking at promises #3 and #4 above, praying the Rosary helps one to live a holy life, which is itself a great sign that a soul is on the road to salvation. (See also paragraphs 381, 488, 600, 2782 in the *Catechism of the Catholic Church*) In fact, St. Louis de Montfort says even more strongly that "an infallible and unmistakable sign by which we can distinguish a heretic, a man of false doctrine, an enemy of God, from one of God's true friends is that the hardened sinner and heretic show nothing but contempt and indifference to Our Lady..." [*True Devotion to Mary*, #30]

Reminder: these promises mean that, by faithfully and devoutly praying the Rosary, Our Lady will obtain for us the necessary Graces to obtain said promises. It is still up to each individual soul to respond to those Graces in order to obtain salvation.

The Origin and History of the Rosary

> "The rosary is the book of the blind, where souls see and there enact the greatest drama of love the world has ever known; it is the book for the simple, which initiates them into mysteries and knowledge more satisfying than the education of other men; it is the book for the aged, whose eyes close upon the shadow of this world, and open on the substance of the next. The power of the rosary is beyond description."
> —Venerable Fulton J. Sheen

The Rosary, or the "Crown of Roses" as it has been called, is largely attributed to St. Dominic, the founder of the Dominican Order. St. Dominic was battling against the Albigensian heresy in the south of France, a region called Languedoc. The Albigensian heresy was a form of dualism in which the material world was evil, while the spiritual world was good. Further, the body was evil, while the soul was good. They believed that adultery, fornication, and even suicide (as a means of freeing the soul from the body) were all praiseworthy. This is not unlike our current "Culture of Death."

St. Dominic preached the truths of the Faith, and was jeered, insulted, and pelted with stones as he traveled. We have the following account from P. Cornelius de Snecka, a disciple of the French Dominican Alan de la Roche:

> We read that at the time when he was preaching to the Albigenses, St. Dominic at first obtained but scanty success: and that one day, complaining of this in pious prayer to our

Blessed Lady, she deigned to reply to him, saying: 'Wonder not that you have obtained so little fruit by your labors, you have spent them on barren soil, not yet watered with the dew of Divine grace. When God willed to re-new the face of the earth, He began by send-ing down on it the fertilizing rain of the An-gelic Salutation. Therefore preach my Psalter composed of 150 Angelic Salutations and 15 Our Fathers, and you will obtain an abundant harvest.'

The Dominican Order holds that the Blessed Mother re-vealed the Rosary to St. Dominic in the church of Prouille in 1208. This was affirmed by Pope Leo XIII and subsequent popes.

Armed now with the Rosary, St. Dominic went into the vil-lages of the heretics and preached the Mysteries of salvation, as the Virgin had instructed. He soon proved an unstoppable evangelizer and the whole south of France was purged of heresy. The late Dominican Reginald Garrigou-Lagrange, a teacher of Pope Saint John Paul II when he was a student at the Angelicum in Rome, stated: "Our Blessed Lady made known to St. Dominic a kind of preaching till then unknown; which she said would be one of the most powerful weapons against future errors and in future difficulties."

Pope Pius V established the Joyful, Sorrowful, and Glorious Mysteries. Pope Saint John Paul the Great later established the Luminous Mysteries in 2002. Each of these "illuminat-ing" mysteries, echo the words of the Blessed Mother at the Wedding at Cana: "Do whatever He tells you."

The Rosary & The Battle of Lepanto

After Constantinople fell to the Ottoman Turks in 1453, the Muslims invaded Hungary and the Balkans and began raiding the coast of Italy. With the control of the Mediterranean at stake, Pope Pius V organized a fleet under Don Juan of Austria, half-brother of Spain's King Philip II. All Christians were implored to pray the rosary, asking Christ to deliver victory to the outnumbered Christian fleet. The scales of power were clearly in favor of the Muslim fleet, with its 251 ships and 82,000 sailors, oarsmen, and soldiers, compared to the Christian fleet of 212 ships and 50,000 sailors, oarsmen, and soldiers.

Before departing Genoa to rally the Holy League fleet at Messina, Don Juan adorned his fleet with the blue Holy League banner, depicting Christ Crucified. Also, the Archbishop of Mexico had given an exact replica of Our Lady of Guadalupe to King Philip II, who passed it on to Andrea Doria, one of the fleet's three principal admirals. Just before The Holy League Navy made contact with the Ottoman forces in the Ionian Sea, the winds shifted dramatically to favor the Holy League, forcing the Turks to rely on oar power while the Holy League was able to maneuver freely.

As the battle raged, the two flagships were both in the front of their center formations. The sailors of Don Juan's flagship *Real* held weapons in one hand and a rosary in the other as they prepared to grapple alongside the Ottoman flagship *Sultana*. The Turks prepared for collision with all the yelling, screaming, and banging they could muster, being met by prayerful silence from the *Real*. As the *Sultana* troops tried to board the *Real* unopposed, they were caught in netting and made to absorb withering gunfire of the Spanish infantry. As both sides flooded the tangled ships with reinforcements, nearly 800 men fought shoulder to shoulder on the bloody decks. Don Juan was wounded by a Muslim arrow, while the Ottoman Commander, Ali Pasha, was killed by a musket ball to the head. Seeing their commander dead on the quarterdeck, the Muslims' morale was destroyed and the banner of their prophet was removed from the masthead of the *Sultana*, replaced with a papal banner. Soon after the capture of their flagship, all the Ottoman ships in the center formation were sunk. In all, 50 Ottoman ships were sunk and 137 more captured with over 30,000 dead, compared to 20 Christian ships sunk and another 30 scuttled due to damage and 7,500 dead. Fifteen thousand Christian prisoners were freed from Turkish ships, having been earlier victims of Muslim raids.

The victory prompted Pope St Pius V to establish the feast of Our Lady of Victory, to give thanks to the Lord for all of his blessings, but also to remember the victory and the powerful intercession of our Blessed Mother.

III.

IMPORTANT

PRAYERS &

NOVENAS

DAILY PRAYERS

The Morning Offering

O Jesus,
through the Immaculate Heart of Mary,
I offer You my prayers, works, joys and sufferings of this day
for all the intentions
of Your Sacred Heart,
in union with the Holy Sacrifice of the Mass
throughout the world,
in reparation for my sins,
for the intentions of all my relatives and friends,
and in particular for the intentions of the Holy Father.
Amen.

The Daily Examen for Midday
Also called "The Examen of Consciousness"

1. Become aware of God's presence.
2. Review the day with gratitude.
3. Pay attention to your emotions.
4. Choose one feature of the day and pray from it.
5. Look toward tomorrow.

For more information, check out
www.ignatianspirituality.com.

Traditional Prayers

The Anima Christi

Soul of Christ, sanctify me.
Body of Christ, save me.
Blood of Christ, inebriate me.
Water from the side of Christ, wash me.
Passion of Christ, strengthen me.
O Good Jesus, hear me.
Within your wounds hide me.
Permit me not to be separated from you.
From the wicked foe, defend me.
At the hour of my death, call me
and bid me come to you
That with your saints I may praise you
For ever and ever. Amen.

The Suscipe of St. Ignatius of Loyola

Take, Lord, and receive all my liberty,

my memory, my understanding,
and my entire will,
All I have and call my own.
You have given all to me.
To you, Lord, I return it.
Everything is yours; do with it what you will.
Give me only your love and your grace,
that is enough for me.

Prayer to St. Michael

St. Michael the Archangel, defend us in battle;
be our defense
against the wickedness and snares of the devil.
May God rebuke him, we humbly pray;
and do you, O prince of the heavenly host,
by the power of God,
thrust into hell Satan and the other evil spirits
who prowl about the world for the ruin of souls.
Amen.

Holy Spirit Prayer of Saint Augustine

Breathe in me, O Holy Spirit,
That my thoughts may all be holy.
Act in me, O Holy Spirit,
That my work, too, may be holy.
Draw my heart, O Holy Spirit,
That I love but what is holy.
Strengthen me, O Holy Spirit,
To defend all that is holy.
Guard me, then, O Holy Spirit,
That I always may be holy.

Memorare Prayer & St. Teresa of Calcutta Emergency Novena*

Remember O most loving Virgin Mary that never was it known in any age that anyone who fled to your protection, implored your help or sought your intercession was left unaided, inspired by this confidence, therefore I fly to thee O Virgin of Virgins my Mother, to you do I come, before you I stand sinful and sorrowful, do not O Mother of the Word Incarnate despise my prayers but in thy mercy graciously hear and answer them. Amen.

*The **Saint Teresa Emergency Novena** simply consists of the Memorare prayer said nine times in a row for an intention.

Angelus

The Angel of the Lord declared to Mary: And she conceived of the Holy Spirit.

> Hail Mary, full of grace, the Lord is with thee; blessed art thou among women and blessed is the fruit of thy womb, Jesus. Holy Mary, Mother of God, pray for us sinners, now and at the hour of our death. Amen.

Behold the handmaid of the Lord: Be it done unto me according to Thy word.

> Hail Mary . . .

And the Word was made Flesh: And dwelt among us.

> Hail Mary . . .

Pray for us, O Holy Mother of God, that we may be made worthy of the promises of Christ.

Let us pray:

> Pour forth, we beseech Thee, O Lord, Thy grace into our hearts; that we, to whom the incarnation of Christ, Thy Son, was made known by the message of an angel, may by His Passion and Cross be brought to the glory of His Resurrection, through the same Christ Our Lord.

Amen.

A Prayer for Detachment

I beg of you, my Lord,
to remove anything that separates
me from you, and you from me.

Remove anything that takes me apart
from your sight, your speech and conversation,
from your benevolence and love.

Cast from me every evil
that stands in the way of my seeing you
hearing, tasting, savoring, and touching you;
knowing, trusting, loving, and possessing you;
of being conscious of your presence
and as far as may be, enjoying you. Amen

from **Blessed Peter Faber SJ** (1506-1546)
An original companion of Saint Ignatius and
gifted director of the Spiritual Exercises

Litany of Humility

O Jesus! meek and humble of heart, **Hear me.**
From the desire of being esteemed,
Deliver me, Jesus.

From the desire of being loved...
From the desire of being extolled ...
From the desire of being honored ...
From the desire of being praised ...
From the desire of being preferred to others...
From the desire of being consulted ...
From the desire of being approved ...
From the fear of being humiliated ...
From the fear of being despised...
From the fear of suffering rebukes ...
From the fear of being calumniated ...
From the fear of being forgotten ...
From the fear of being ridiculed ...
From the fear of being wronged ...
From the fear of being suspected ...

That others may be loved more than I,
Jesus, grant me the grace to desire it.

That others may be esteemed more than I ...
That, in the opinion of the world,
others may increase and I may decrease ...
That others may be chosen and I set aside ...
That others may be praised and I unnoticed ...
That others may be preferred to me in everything...
That others may become holier than I, provided that I may
become as holy as I should...

Rafael Cardinal Merry del Val (1865-1930),
Secretary of State for Pope Saint Pius X

POPE FRANCIS' FIVE FINGER PRAYER

1. The thumb is the closest finger to you. So start praying for those who are closest to you. They are the persons easiest to remember. To pray for our dear ones is a "sweet obligation."

2. The next finger is the index. Pray for those who teach you, instruct you and heal you. They need the support and wisdom to show direction to others. Always keep them in your prayers.

3. The following finger is the tallest. It reminds us of our leaders, the governors and those who have authority. They need God's guidance.

4. The fourth finger is the ring finger. Even that it may surprise you, it is our weakest finger. It should remind us to pray for the weakest, the sick or those plagued by problems. They need your prayers.

5. And finally we have our smallest finger, the smallest of all. Your pinkie should remind you to pray for yourself. When you are done praying for the other four groups, you will be able to see your own needs but in the proper perspective, and also you will be able to pray for your own needs in a better way.

Prayers for Purity

From Angelic Warfare Confraternity
Dominican Friars, Province of Saint Joseph
www.AngelicWarfareConfraternity.org/prayers

The Prayer *to* St. Thomas for Purity
Chosen lily of innocence, pure St. Thomas,
who kept chaste the robe of baptism
and became an angel in the flesh
after being girded by two angels,
I implore you to commend me to Jesus, the Spotless Lamb,
and to Mary, the Queen of Virgins.
Gentle protector of my purity, ask them that I,
who wear the holy sign of your victory over the flesh,
may also share your purity,
and after imitating you on earth
may at last come to be crowned with you among the angels.
Amen.

The Prayer *of* St. Thomas for Purity
Dear Jesus, I know that every perfect gift,
and especially that of chastity,
depends on the power of Your providence.
Without You a mere creature can do nothing.
Therefore, I beg You to defend by Your grace
the chastity and purity of my body and soul.
And if I have ever sensed or imagined anything
that could stain my chastity and purity,
blot it out, Supreme Lord of my powers,
that I may advance with a pure heart
in Your love and service,
offering myself on the most pure altar of Your divinity
all the days of my life. Amen.

Fifteen Hail Marys
With Petitions for Chastity

Opening Prayer: Dear Jesus, I know that every perfect gift, and especially that of chastity, depends on the power of Your providence. Without You a mere creature can do nothing. Therefore, I beg You to defend by Your grace the chastity and purity of my body and soul. And if I have ever imagined or felt anything that could stain my chastity and purity, blot it out, Supreme Lord of my powers, that I may advance with a pure heart in Your love and service, offering myself on the most pure altar of Your divinity all the days of my life. Amen.

1. For our social and cultural climate, that it may be purified of everything contrary to chastity, and that we may have the strength to resist the pressures of prevailing ideologies. "In the world you have tribulation; but be of good cheer, I have conquered the world" (Jn. 16:33) "In all these things we are more than conquerors through him who loved us" (Rom. 8:37) **Hail Mary...**

2. For our relationships, that they may holy, healthy, and honorable at all times. "Having purified your souls by your obedience to the truth for a sincere love of the brethren, love one another earnestly from the heart" (1 Pet. 1:22) **Hail Mary...**

3. For modesty in our dress and movement, that the way we dress and carry ourselves may veil the mystery of our being, and that we may have the strength to resist the allurements of fashion and the glamour of sin. "Do not be conformed to this age, but be

transformed by the renewal of your mind" (Rom. 12:2) **Hail Mary...**

4. For our five senses, that the things we see, the music we hear, the food and drink we eat, and the encounters we have through touch may all be pure and holy. "Seek the things that are above" (Col. 3:1) **Hail Mary...**

5. For our sensuality, that our impulses may not be captivated by base pleasures, but freed by wisdom and inflamed for what is good. "In your struggle against sin you have not yet resisted to the point of shedding your blood" (Heb. 12:4) **Hail Mary...**

6. For our imagination, that we may be preserved from any fantasies that defile us, that all impure images may vanish, and that we may be protected from all the assaults of demons. "Be renewed in the spirit of your minds...Put on the whole armor of God" (Eph. 4:23, 6:11) **Hail Mary...**

7. For our memory, that no memories of past experiences may disturb us in any way, but that the Lord may touch and heal us through hope for a better future. "And every one who thus hopes in him purifies himself as he is pure" (1 Jn. 3:1) **Hail Mary...**

8. For our estimation, that we may quickly sense dangers to chastity and instinctively flee from them, that we may never turn away from higher, more difficult, and more honorable goods for the sake of sinful self-indulgence. "Do not lay up for yourselves treasures on earth, where moth and rust consume and where thieves break in and steal, but lay up for yourselves treasures in heaven, where neither moth nor rust consumes and where thieves do not break in and steal." (Mt. 6:19-20) **Hail Mary...**

9. For our affectivity, that we may love chastity and rejoice in it, that all of our emotions may cooperate in its growth, and that no sadness, discouragement, fear, insecurity, or loneliness may afflict us unto sexual sin. "For the grace of God has appeared, saving all and training us to reject godless ways and worldly desires and to live temperately, justly, and devoutly in this age, as we await the blessed hope, the appearance of the glory of the great God and of our savior Jesus Christ" (Titus 2:11-12) **Hail Mary...**

10. For our intellect, that it may be purged of all false beliefs and misunderstandings about human sexuality and that the good angels may flood our intellects with thoughts that are gracious, pure, lovely, honorable, and true. "Finally, brethren, whatever is true, whatever is honorable, whatever is just, whatever is pure, whatever is lovely, whatever is gracious, if there is any excellence, if there is anything worthy of praise, think about these things." (Phil. 4:8) **Hail Mary...**

11. For our will, that it may never be opposed by our sensuality, that it may never be divided or conflicted in the moment, but may hold fast to chastity no matter how difficult it may be. "For the Son of God, Jesus Christ...was not Yes and No; but in him it is always Yes. For all the promises of God find their Yes in him." (2 Cor. 1:19-20) **Hail Mary...**

12. For our conscience, that it may be swift to judge what is the chaste thing to do, swifter to execute it, and wholly preserved from the suggestions of demons. "How much more shall the blood of Christ, who through the eternal Spirit offered himself without blemish to God, purify your conscience from dead

works to serve the living God?" (Heb. 9:14) **Hail Mary...**

13. For our hearts, that the place where Christ abides in us with the Father and the Spirit may become the place where we live with the Holy Trinity in friendship. "Jesus answered him, "If a man loves me, he will keep my word, and my Father will love him, and we will come to him and make our home with him." (Jn. 14:23) **Hail Mary...**

14. For the grace of self-surrender, that we may hand over to the God nothing less than our whole lives. "Father, into your hands I commend my spirit" (Lk. 23:46) "Blessed are the poor in spirit, for theirs in the kingdom of heaven" (Mt. 5:3) **Hail Mary...**

15. For love. "In this is love, not that we loved God but that he loved us and sent his Son to be the expiation for our sins." (1 Jn. 4:10) "But God shows his love for us in that while we were yet sinners Christ died for us" (Rom. 5:8) **Hail Mary...**

Closing Prayer: Heavenly King, Consoler, Spirit of Truth, you who are everywhere present and fill all things, Treasury of all that is good, Choirmaster of Life, Come, dwell within us, cleanse us of all stain, and save our souls O Good One.

MOST POWERFUL NOVENAS

Novena to the Holy Spirit

The tradition of the novena began in the Upper Room where the Apostles gathered with the Blessed Mother for nine days, from the Ascension of Christ to Pentecost, for the coming of the Holy Spirit. Though the following Novena to the Holy Spirit can be prayed at any time, it is recommended that it be said between Ascension and Pentecost. There is, as well, an alternate version of this novena in which one prays for the Seven Gifts of the Holy Spirit.

Novena Prayer:
Dearest Holy Spirit, confiding in Your deep, personal love for me, I am making this novena for the following request, if it be Your Holy Will to grant it:
(State your request).

Teach me, Divine Spirit, to know and seek my last end; grant me the holy fear of God; grant me true contrition and patience. Do not let me fall into sin. Give me an increase of faith, hope and charity, and bring forth in my soul all the virtues proper to my state in life.

Make me a faithful disciple of Jesus and an obedient child of the Church. Give me efficacious grace sufficient to keep the Commandments and to receive the Sacraments worthily. Give me the four Cardinal Virtues, Your Seven Gifts, Your Twelve Fruits. Raise me to perfection in the state of life to which You have called me and lead me through a happy death to everlasting life. I ask this through Christ our Lord, Amen.

Novena to St. Joseph

The Novena for St. Joseph's intercession is acknowledged by many to be the most powerful novena prayer. It can be used in manifold different situations, but it is often used to help a father find employment.

Novena Prayer to be said at the end of each day's specific devotion (included below):

Saint Joseph, I, your unworthy child, greet you. You are the faithful protector and intercessor of all who love and venerate you. You know that I have special confidence in you and that, after Jesus and Mary, I place all my hope of salvation in you, for you are especially powerful with God and will never abandon your faithful servants. Therefore I humbly invoke you and commend myself, with all who are dear to me and all that belong to me, to your intercession. I beg of you, by your love for Jesus and Mary, not to abandon me during life and to assist me at the hour of my death.

Glorious Saint Joseph, spouse of the Immaculate Virgin, obtain for me a pure, humble, charitable mind, and perfect resignation to the divine Will. Be my guide, my father, and my model through life that I may merit to die as you did in the arms of Jesus and Mary.

Loving Saint Joseph, faithful follower of Jesus Christ, I raise my heart to you to implore your powerful intercession in obtaining from the Divine Heart of Jesus all the graces necessary for my spiritual and temporal welfare, particularly the grace of a happy death, and the special grace I now implore:

(State your request)

Guardian of the Word Incarnate, I feel confident that your prayers in my behalf will be graciously heard before the throne of God. Amen.

[Pray the Memorare]

Day One
FOSTER-FATHER OF JESUS

Saint Joseph, you were privileged to share in the mystery of the Incarnation as the foster-father of Jesus. Mary alone was directly connected with the fulfillment of the mystery, in that she gave her consent to Christ's conception and allowed the Holy Spirit to form the sacred humanity of Jesus from her blood. You had a part in this mystery in an indirect manner, by fulfilling the condition necessary for the Incarnation -- the protection of Mary's virginity before and during your married life with her. You made the virginal marriage possible, and this was a part of God's plan, foreseen, willed, and decreed from all eternity.

In a more direct manner you shared in the support, upbringing, and protection of the Divine Child as His foster-father. For this purpose the Heavenly Father gave you a genuine heart of a father -- a heart full of love and self-sacrifice. With the toil of your hands you were obliged to offer protection to the Divine Child, to procure for Him food, clothing, and a home. You were truly the saint of the holy childhood of Jesus -- the living created providence which watched over the Christ-Child.

When Herod sought the Child to put Him to death, the Heavenly Father sent an angel but only as a messenger, giving orders for the flight; the rest He left entirely in your hands. It was that fatherly love which was the only refuge that received and protected the Divine Child. Your fatherly love carried Him through the desert into Egypt until all enemies were removed. Then on your arms the Child returned to Nazareth to be nourished and provided for during many years by the labor of your hands. Whatever a human son owes to a human father for all the benefits of his up-bringing and support, Jesus owed to you, because you were to Him a foster-father, teacher, and protector.

You served the Divine Child with a singular love. God gave you a heart filled with heavenly, supernatural love -- a love far deeper and more powerful than any natural father's love could be.

You served the Divine Child with great unselfishness, without any regard to self-interest, but not without sacrifices. You did not toil for yourself, but you seemed to be an instrument intended for the benefit of others, to be put aside as soon as it had done its word, for you disappeared from the scene once the childhood of Jesus had passed.

You were the shadow of the Heavenly Father not only as the earthly representative of the authority of the Father, but also by means of your fatherhood -- which only appeared to be natural -- you were to hide for a while the divinity of Jesus. What a wonderfully sublime and divine vocation was yours -- the loving Child which you carried in your arms, and loved and served so faithfully, had God in Heaven as Father and was Himself God!

Yours is a very special rank among the saints of the Kingdom of God, because you were so much a part of the very life of the Word of God made Man. In your house at Nazareth and under your care the redemption of mankind was prepared. What you accomplished, you did for us. You are not only a powerful and great saint in the Kingdom of God, but a benefactor of the whole of Christendom and mankind. Your rank in the Kingdom of God, surpassing far in dignity and honor of all the angels, deserves our very special veneration, love, and gratitude.

Saint Joseph, I thank God for your privilege of having been chosen by God to be the foster-father of His Divine Son. As a token of your own gratitude to God for this your greatest privilege, obtain for me the grace of a very devoted love for Jesus Christ, my God and my Savior. Help me to serve Him with some of the self-sacrificing love and devotion which you had while on this earth with Him. Grant that through your intercession with Jesus, your foster-Son, I may reach the degree of holiness God has destined for me, and save my soul.

[Say the NOVENA PRAYER]

Second Day
VIRGINAL HUSBAND OF MARY

Saint Joseph, I honor you as the true husband of Mary. Scripture says: "Jacob begot Joseph, the husband of Mary, and of her was born Jesus who is called Christ" (Matt. 1:16). Your marriage to Mary was a sacred contract by which you and Mary gave yourselves to each other. Mary really belonged to you with all she was and had. You had a right to her love and obedience; and no other person so won her esteem, obedience, and love.

You were also the protector and witness of Mary's virginity. By your marriage you gave to each other your virginity, and also the mutual right over it -- a right to safeguard the other's virtue. This mutual virginity also belonged to the divine plan of the Incarnation, for God sent His angel to assure you that motherhood and virginity in Mary could be united.

This union of marriage not only brought you into daily familiar association with Mary, the loveliest of God's creatures, but also enabled you to share with her a mutual exchange of spiritual goods. And Mary found her edification in your calm, humble, and deep virtue, purity, and sanctity. What a great honor comes to you from this close union with her whom the Son of God calls Mother and whom He declared the Queen of heaven and earth! Whatever Mary had belonged by right to you also, and this included her Son, even though He had been given to her by God in a wonderful way. Jesus belonged to you as His legal father. Your marriage was the way which God chose to have Jesus introduced into the world, a great divine mystery from which all benefits have come to us.

God the Son confided the guardianship and the support of His Immaculate Mother to your care. Mary's life was that of the Mother of the Savior, who did not come upon earth to enjoy honors and pleasures, but to redeem the world by hard work, suffering, and the cross. You were the faithful companion, support, and comforter of the Mother of Sorrows. How loyal you were to her in poverty, journeying, work, and pain. Your love for Mary was based upon your esteem for her as Mother of God. After God and the Divine Child, you loved no one as much as her. Mary responded to this love. She submitted to your guidance with naturalness and easy grace and childlike confidence. The Holy Spirit Himself was the bond of the great love which united your hearts.

Saint Joseph, I thank God for your privilege of being the virginal husband of Mary. As a token of your own gratitude to God, obtain for me the grace to love Jesus with all my heart, as you did, and love Mary with some of the tenderness and loyalty with which you loved her.

[Say the NOVENA PRAYER]

Third Day
MAN CHOSEN BY THE BLESSED TRINITY

Saint Joseph, you were the man chosen by God the Father. He selected you to be His representative on earth, hence He granted you all the graces and blessings you needed to be His worthy representative.

You were the man chosen by God the Son. Desirous of a worthy foster-father, He added His own riches and gifts, and above all, His love. The true measure of your sanctity is to be judged by your imitation of Jesus. You were entirely consecrated to Jesus, working always near Him, offering Him your virtues, your work, your sufferings, your very life. Jesus lived in you perfectly so that you were transformed into Him. In this lies your special glory, and the keynote of your sanctity. Hence, after Mary, you are the holiest of the saints.

You were chosen by the Holy Spirit. He is the mutual Love of the Father and the Son -- the heart of the Holy Trinity. In His wisdom He draws forth all creatures from nothing, guides them to their end in showing them their destiny and giving them the means to reach it. Every vocation and every fulfillment of a vocation proceeds from the Holy Spirit. As a foster-father of Jesus and head of the Holy Family, you had an exalted and most responsible vocation -- to open the way for the redemption of the world and to prepare for it by the education and guidance of the youth of the God-Man. In this work you cooperated as the instrument of the Holy Spirit. The Holy Spirit was the guide; you obeyed and carried out the works. How perfectly you obeyed the guidance of the God of Love!

The words of the Old Testament which Pharaoh spoke concerning Joseph of Egypt can well be applied to you: "Can we find such another man, that is full of the spirit of God, or a wise man like to him?" (Gen. 41:38). No less is your share in the divine work of God than was that of Egypt. You now reign with your foster-Son and see reflected in the mirror of God's Wisdom the Divine Will and what is of benefit to our souls.

Saint Joseph, I thank God for having made you the man specially chosen by Him. As a token of your own gratitude to God, obtain for me the grace to imitate your virtues so that I too may be pleasing to the Heart of God. Help me to give myself entirely to His service and to the accomplishment of His Holy Will, that one day I may reach heaven and be eternally united to God as you are.

[Say the NOVENA PRAYER]

Fourth Day
FAITHFUL SERVANT

Saint Joseph, you lived for one purpose -- to be the personal servant of Jesus Christ, the Word made flesh. Your noble birth and ancestry, the graces and gifts, so generously poured out on you by God -- all this was yours to serve our Lord better. Every thought, word, and action of yours was a homage to the love and glory of the Incarnate Word. You fulfilled most faithfully the role of a good and faithful servant who cared for the House of God.

How perfect was your obedience! Your position in the Holy Family obliged you to command, but besides being the foster-father of Jesus, you were also His disciple. For almost thirty years, you watched the God-Man display a simple and prompt obedience, and you grew to love and practice it very perfectly yourself. Without exception you submitted to God, to the civil rulers, and to the voice of your conscience.

When God sent an angel to tell you to care for Mary, you obeyed in spite of the mystery which surrounded her moth-

56

erhood. When you were told to flee into Egypt under painful conditions, you obeyed without the slightest word of complaint. When God advised you in a dream to return to Nazareth, you obeyed. In every situation your obedience was as simple as your faith, as humble as your heart, as prompt as your love. It neglected nothing; it took in every command.

You had the virtue of perfect devotedness, which marks a good servant. Every moment of your life was consecrated to the service of our Lord: sleep, rest, work, pain. Faithful to your duties, you sacrificed everything unselfishly, even cheerfully. You would have sacrificed even the happiness of being with Mary. The rest and quiet of Nazareth was sacrificed at the call of duty. Your entire life was one generous giving, even to the point of being ready to die in proof of your love for Jesus and Mary. With true unselfish devotedness you worked without praise or reward.

But God wanted you to be in a certain sense a cooperator in the Redemption of the world. He confided to you the care of nourishing and defending the Divine Child. He wanted you to be poor and to suffer because He destined you to be the foster-father of His Son, who came into the world to save men by His sufferings and death, and you were to share in His suffering. In all of these important tasks, the Heavenly Father always found you a faithful servant!

Saint Joseph, I thank God for your privilege of being God's faithful servant. As a token of your own gratitude to God, obtain for me the grace to be a faithful servant of God as you were. Help me to share, as you did, the perfect obedience of Jesus, who came not to do His Will, but the Will of His Father; to trust in the Providence of God, knowing that if I do His Will, He will provide for all my needs of soul and body; to be calm in my trials and to leave it to our Lord to free me from them when it pleases Him to do so. And help me to imitate your generosity, for there can be no greater reward here on earth than the joy and honor of being a faithful servant of God.

[Say the NOVENA PRAYER]

Fifth Day
PATRON OF THE CHURCH

Saint Joseph, God has appointed you patron of the Catholic Church because you were the head of the Holy Family, the starting-point of the Church. You were the father, protector, guide and support of the Holy Family. For that reason you belong in a particular way to the Church, which was the purpose of the Holy Family's existence.

I believe that the Church is the family of God on earth. Its government is represented in priestly authority which consists above all in its power over the true Body of Christ, really present in the Blessed Sacrament of the Altar, thus continuing Christ's life in the Church. From this power, too, comes authority over the Mystical Body of Christ, the members of the Church -- the power to teach and govern souls, to reconcile them with God, to bless them, and to pray for them.

You have a special relationship to the priesthood because you possessed a wonderful power over our Savior Himself. Your life and office were of a priestly function and are especially connected with the Blessed Sacrament. To some extent you were the means of bringing the Redeemer to us -- as it is the priest's function to bring Him to us in the Mass -- for you reared Jesus, supported, nourished, protected and sheltered Him. You were prefigured by the patriarch Joseph, who kept supplies of wheat for his people. But how much greater than he were you! Joseph of old gave the Egyptians mere bread for their bodies. You nourished, and with the most tender care, preserved for the Church Him who is the Bread of Heaven and who gives eternal life in Holy Communion.

God has appointed you patron of the Church because the glorious title of patriarch also falls by special right to you. The patriarchs were the heads of families of the Chosen People, and theirs was the honor to prepare for the Savior's incarnation. You belonged to this line of patriarchs, for you were one of the last descendants of the family of David and one of the nearest forebears of Christ according to the flesh. As husband of Mary, the Mother of God, and as the foster-father of the Savior, you were directly connected with Christ.

58

Your vocation was especially concerned with the Person of Jesus; your entire activity centered about Him. You are, therefore, the closing of the Old Testament and the beginning of the New, which took its rise with the Holy Family of Nazareth. Because the New Testament surpasses the Old in every respect, you are the patriarch of patriarchs, the most venerable, exalted, and amiable of all the patriarchs.

Through Mary, the Church received Christ, and therefore the Church is indebted to her. But the Church owes her debt of gratitude and veneration to you also, for you were the chosen one who enabled Christ to enter into the world according to the laws of order and fitness. It was by you that the patriarchs and the prophets and the faithful reaped the fruit of God's promise. Alone among them all, you saw with your own eyes and possessed the Redeemer promised to the rest of men.

Saint Joseph, I thank God for your privilege of being the Patron of the Church. As a token of your own gratitude to God, obtain for me the grace to live always as a worthy member of this Church, so that through it I may save my soul. Bless the priests, the religious, and the laity of the Catholic Church, that they may ever grow in God's love and faithfulness in His service. Protect the Church from the evils of our day and from the persecution of her enemies. Through your powerful intercession may the church successfully accomplish its mission in this world -- the glory of God and the salvation of souls!

[Say the NOVENA PRAYER]

Sixth Day
PATRON OF FAMILIES

Saint Joseph, I venerate you as the gentle head of the Holy Family. The Holy Family was the scene of your life's work in its origin, in its guidance, in its protection, in your labor for Jesus and Mary, and even in your death in their arms. You lived, moved, and acted in the loving company of Jesus and Mary. The inspired writer describes your life at Nazareth in only a few words: "And (Jesus) went down with them and came to Nazareth, and was subject to them" (Luke, 2:51). Yet these words tell of your high vocation here on earth, and the abundance of graces which filled your soul during those years spent in Nazareth.

Your family life at Nazareth was all radiant with the light of divine charity. There was an intimate union of heart and mind among the members of your Holy Family. There could not have been a closer bond than that uniting you to Jesus, your foster-Son and to Mary, your most loving wife. Jesus chose to fulfill toward you, His foster-father, all the duties of a faithful son, showing you every mark of honor and affection due to a parent. And Mary showed you all the signs of respect and love of a devoted wife. You responded to this love and veneration from Jesus and Mary with feelings of deepest love and respect. You had for Jesus a true fatherly love, enkindled and kept aglow in your heart by the Holy Spirit. And you could not cease to admire the workings of grace in Mary's soul, and this admiration caused the holy love which you had consecrated to her on the day of your wedding grow stronger every day.

God has made you a heavenly patron of family life because you sanctified yourself as head of the Holy Family and thus by your beautiful example sanctified family life. How peacefully and happily the Holy Family rested under the care of your fatherly rule, even in the midst of trials. You were the protector, counselor, and consolation of the Holy Family in every need. And just as you were the model of piety, so you gave us by your zeal, your earnestness and devout trust in God's providence, and especially by your love, the example of labor according to the Will of God. You cherished all the experiences common to family life and the sacred memories of the life, sufferings, and joys in the company of Jesus and Mary. Therefore the family is dear to you as the work of God, and it is of the highest importance in your eyes to promote the honor of God and the well-being of man. In your loving fatherliness and unfailing intercession you are the patron and intercessor of families, and you deserve a place in every home.

Saint Joseph, I thank God for your privilege of living in the Holy Family and being its head. As a token of your own gratitude to God, obtain God's blessing upon my own family. Make our home the kingdom of Jesus and Mary -- a kingdom of peace, of joy, and love.

I also pray for all Christian families. Your help is needed in our day when God's enemy has directed his attack against the family in order to desecrate and destroy it. In the face of these evils, as patron of families, be pleased to help; and as of old, you arose to save the Child and His Mother, so today arise to protect the sanctity of the home. Make our homes sanctuaries of prayer, of love, of patient sacrifice, and of work. May they be modeled after your own at Nazareth. Remain with us with Jesus and Mary, so that by your help we may obey the commandments of God and of the Church; receive the holy sacraments of God and of the Church; live a life of prayer; and foster religious instruction in our homes. Grant that we may be reunited in God's Kingdom and eternally live in the company of the Holy Family in heaven.

[Say the NOVENA PRAYER]

Seventh Day
PATRON OF WORKERS

Saint Joseph, you devoted your time at Nazareth to the work of a carpenter. It was the Will of God that you and your foster-Son should spend your days together in manual labor. What a beautiful example you set for the working classes!

It was especially for the poor, who compose the greater part of mankind, that Jesus came upon earth, for in the synagogue of Nazareth, He read the words of Isaiah and referred them to Himself: "The Spirit of the Lord is upon me, because He has anointed Me to bring good news to the poor..." (Luke 4:18). It was God's Will that you should be occupied with work common to poor people, that in this way Jesus Himself might ennoble it by inheriting it from you, His foster-father, and by freely embracing it. Thus our Lord teaches us that for the humbler class of workmen, He has in store His richest graces, provided they live content in the place God's Providence has assigned them, and remain poor in spirit for He said, "Blessed are the poor in spirit, for theirs is the kingdom of heaven" (Matt. 5:3).

The kind of work to which you devoted your time in the workshop of Nazareth offered you many occasions of practicing humility. You were privileged to see each day the example of humility which Jesus practiced -- a virtue most pleasing to Him. He chose for His earthly surroundings not the courts of princes nor the halls of the learned, but a little workshop of Nazareth. Here you shared for many years the humble and hidden toiling of the God-Man. What a touching example for the worker of today!

While your hands were occupied with manual work, your mind was turned to God in prayer. From the Divine Master, who worked along with you, you learned to work in the presence of God in the spirit of prayer, for as He worked He adored His Father and recommended the welfare of the world to Him, Jesus also instructed you in the wonderful truths of grace and virtue, for you were in close contact with Him who said of Himself, "I am the Way and the Truth and the Life."

As you were working at your trade, you were reminded of the greatness and majesty of God, who, as a most wise Architect, formed this vast universe with wonderful skill and limitless power.

The light of divine faith that filled your mind, did not grow dim when you saw Jesus working as a carpenter. You firmly believed that the saintly Youth working beside you was truly God's own Son.

Saint Joseph, I thank God for your privilege of being able to work side by side with Jesus in the carpenter shop of Nazareth. As a token of your own gratitude to God, obtain for me the grace to respect the dignity of labor and ever to be content with the position in life, however lowly, in which it may please Divine Providence to place me. Teach me to work for God and with God in the spirit of humility and prayer, as you did, so that I may offer my toil in union with the sacrifice of Jesus in the Mass as a reparation for my sins, and gain rich merit for heaven.

[Say the NOVENA PRAYER]

Eighth Day
FRIEND IN SUFFERING

Saint Joseph, your share of suffering was very great because of your close union with the Divine Savior. All the mysteries of His life were more or less mysteries of suffering. Poverty pressed upon you, and the cross of labor followed you everywhere. Nor were you spared domestic crosses, owing to misunderstandings in regard to the holiest and most cherished of all beings, Jesus and Mary, who were all to you. Keen must have been the suffering caused by the uncertainty regarding Mary's virginity; by the bestowal of the name of Jesus, which pointed to future misfortune. Deeply painful must have been the prophecy of Simeon, the flight into Egypt, the disappearance of Jesus at the Paschal feast. To these sufferings were surely added interior sorrow at the sight of the sins of your own people.

You bore all this suffering in a truly Christ-like manner, and in this you are our example. No sound of complaint or impatience escaped you -- you were, indeed, the silent saint! You submitted to all in the spirit of faith, humility, confidence, and love. You cheerfully bore all in union with and for the Savior and His Mother, knowing well that true love is a crucified love. But God never forsook you in your trials. The trials, too, disappeared and were changed at last into consolation and joy.

It seems that God had purposely intended your life to be filled with suffering as well as consolation to keep before my eyes the truth that my life on earth is but a succession of joys and sorrows, and that I must gratefully accept whatever God sends me, and during the time of consolation prepare for suffering. Teach me to bear my cross in the spirit of faith, of confidence, and of gratitude toward God. In a happy eternity, I shall thank God fervently for the sufferings which He deigned to send me during my pilgrimage on earth, and which after your example I endured with patience and heartfelt love for Jesus and Mary.

You were truly the martyr of the hidden life. This was God's Will, for the holier a person is, the more he is tried for the love and glory of God. If suffering is the flowering of God's grace in a soul and the triumph of the soul's love for God, being the greatest of saints after Mary, you suffered more than any of the martyrs.

Because you have experienced the sufferings of this valley of tears, you are most kind and sympathetic toward those in need. Down through the ages souls have turned to you in distress and have always found you a faithful friend in suffering. You have graciously heard their prayers in their needs even though it demanded a miracle. Having been so intimately united with Jesus and Mary in life, your intercession with Them is most powerful.

Saint Joseph, I thank God for your privilege of being able to suffer for Jesus and Mary. As a token of your own gratitude to God, obtain for me the grace to bear my suffering patiently for love of Jesus and Mary. Grant that I may unite the sufferings, works and disappointments of life with the sacrifice of Jesus in the Mass, and share like you in Mary's spirit of sacrifice.

[Say the NOVENA PRAYER]

Ninth Day
PATRON OF A HAPPY DEATH

Saint Joseph, how fitting it was that at the hour of your death Jesus should stand at your bedside with Mary, the sweetness and hope of all mankind. You gave your entire life to the service of Jesus and Mary; at death you enjoyed the consolation of dying in Their loving arms. You accepted death in the spirit of loving submission to the Will of God, and this acceptance crowned your hidden life of virtue. Yours was a merciful judgment, for your foster-Son, for whom you had cared so lovingly, was your Judge, and Mary was your advocate. The verdict of the Judge was a word of encouragement to wait for His coming to Limbo, where He would shower you with the choicest fruits of the Redemption, and an embrace of grateful affection before you breathed forth your soul into eternity.

64

You looked into eternity and to your everlasting reward with confidence. If our Savior blessed the shepherds, the Magi, Simeon, John the Baptist, and others, because they greeted His presence with devoted hearts for a brief passing hour, how much more did He bless you who have sanctified yourself for so many years in His company and that of His Mother? If Jesus regards every corporal and spiritual work of mercy, performed in behalf of our fellow men out of love for Him, as done to Himself, and promises heaven as a reward, what must have been the extent of His gratitude to you who in the truest sense of the word have received Him, given Him shelter, clothed, nourished, and consoled Him at the sacrifice of your strength and rest, and even your life, with a love which surpassed the love of all fathers.

God really and personally made Himself your debtor. Our Divine Savior paid that debt of gratitude by granting you many graces in your lifetime, especially the grace of growing in love, which is the best and most perfect of all gifts. Thus at the end of your life your heart became filled with love, the fervor and longing of which your frail body could not resist. Your soul followed the triumphant impulse of your love and winged its flight from earth to bear the prophets and patriarchs in Limbo the glad tidings of the advent of the Redeemer.

Saint Joseph, I thank God for your privilege of being able to die in the arms of Jesus and Mary. As a token of your own gratitude to God, obtain for me the grace of a happy death. Help me to spend each day in preparation for death. May I, too, accept death in the spirit of resignation to God's Holy Will, and die, as you did, in the arms of Jesus, strengthened by Holy Viaticum, and in the arms of Mary, with her rosary in my hand and her name on my lips!

[Say the NOVENA PRAYER]

Novena to St. Jude

The Novena is said for St. Jude's intercession in desperate situations and hopeless cases. Pray the following Novena Prayer plus an Our Father and a Hail Mary for nine consecutive days.

Novena Prayer:
Most holy Apostle, St. Jude, faithful servant and friend of Jesus, the Church honors and invokes you universally, as the patron of difficult cases, of things almost despaired of, Pray for me, I am so helpless and alone.

Intercede with God for me that He bring visible and speedy help where help is almost despaired of. Come to my assistance in this great need that I may receive the consolation and help of heaven in all my necessities, tribulations, and sufferings – particularly *(state your request)* – and that I may praise God with you and all the saints forever. I promise, O Blessed St. Jude, to be ever mindful of this great favor granted me by God and to always honor you as my special and powerful patron, and to gratefully encourage devotion to you. Amen.

May the Most Sacred Heart of Jesus be adored, and loved in all the tabernacles until the end of time. Amen.
May the most Sacred Heart of Jesus be praised and glorified now and forever. Amen
St. Jude pray for us and hear our prayers. Amen.

Blessed be the Sacred Heart of Jesus
Blessed be the Immaculate Heart of Mary
Blessed be St. Jude Thaddeus, in all the world and for all Eternity.

The Novena Prayer is followed by an Our Father and a Hail Mary.

Novena to Our Lady, Undoer of Knots

In *Against Heresies*, St. Irenaeus of Lyons observed that "the knot of Eve's disobedience was loosed by the obedience of Mary. For what the virgin Eve had bound fast through unbelief, this did the Virgin Mary set free through faith."

The artist Johann Melchior Georg Schmittdner painted "Mary Undoer of Knots" sometime around the year 1700. Mary is depicted standing on the crescent moon, which symbolizes her Immaculate Conception, as well as a knotted serpent. The painting has been venerated since the eighteenth century in the Church of St. Peter in Perlack, Augsburg, Germany.

Devotion to "Our Lady, Undoer of Knots" has been growing in popularity in the rest of the world ever since a student brought a postcard of the painting back with him to Argentina in the 1980s. That student was Jesuit priest Jorge Mario Bergoglio, who has since become Pope Francis I. The pope maintains a personal devotion to Our Lady, Undoer of Knots.

So, what are these knots? These knots are the seemingly insurmountable problems of our lives. Is your family estranged from itself? Do you see no possible way your loved one will return to the Church? Are you or a loved one wrestling with an addiction? ***Bring these knots to Christ through the Blessed Mother.*** Even the thorniest of knots will unravel at her touch.

The text of the following novena comes from the "Pray More Novenas" website (www.praymorenovenas.com).

After each day's particular invocation of the Blessed Mother, pray the following:

Mary, Undoer of Knots, pray for me.

Virgin Mary, Mother of fair love, Mother who never refuses to come to the aid of a child in need, Mother whose hands never cease to serve your beloved children because they are moved by the divine love and immense mercy that exist in your heart, cast your compassionate eyes upon me and see the snarl of knots that exists in my life. You know very well how desperate I am, my pain, and how I am bound by these knots. Mary, Mother to whom God entrusted the undoing of the knots in the lives of his children, I entrust into your hands the ribbon of my life. No one, not even the evil one himself, can take it away from your precious care. In your hands there is no knot that cannot be undone. Powerful Mother, by your grace and intercessory power with Your Son and My Liberator, Jesus, take into your hands today this knot.

[Mention your request here]

I beg you to undo it for the glory of God, once for all. You are my hope.
O my Lady, you are the only consolation God gives me, the fortification of my feeble strength, the enrichment of my destitution, and, with Christ, the freedom from my chains. Hear my plea.
Keep me, guide me, protect me, o safe refuge!

Mary, Undoer of Knots, pray for me. Amen.

Day 1:
Dearest Holy Mother, Most Holy Mary, you undo the knots that suffocate your children. Extend your merciful hands to me. I entrust to You today this knot [mention your request here] and all the negative consequences that it provokes in my life.

Day 2:
Mary, Beloved Mother, channel of all grace, I return to You today my heart, recognizing that I am a sinner in need of your help. I entrust into Your hands this knot [mention your request here] which keeps me from reflecting the glory of God.

Day 3:
Meditating Mother, Queen of heaven, in whose hands the treasures of the King are found, turn your merciful eyes upon me today. I entrust into your holy hands this knot in my life [mention your request here] and all the rancor and resentment it has caused in me.

Day 4:
Dearest Holy Mother, you are generous with all who seek you, have mercy on me. I entrust into your hands this knot which robs the peace of my heart, paralyzes my soul and keeps me from going to my Lord and serving Him with my life.

Day 5:
Mother, Undoer of Knots, generous and compassionate, I come to You today to once again entrust this knot [mention your request here] in my life to you and to ask the divine wisdom to undo, under the light of the Holy Spirit, this snarl of problems.

Day 6:
Queen of Mercy, I entrust to you this knot in my life [mention your request here] and I ask you to give me a heart that is patient until you undo it.

Day 7:
Mother Most Pure, I come to You today to beg you to undo this knot in my life [mention your request here] and free me from the snares of evil.

69

Day 8:

Virgin Mother of God, overflowing with mercy, have mercy on your child and undo this knot [mention your request here] in my life.

Day 9:

Most Holy Mary, our Advocate, Undoer of Knots, I come today to thank you for undoing this knot in my life.

You know very well the suffering it has caused me. Thank you for coming, Mother, with your long fingers of mercy to dry the tears in my eyes; you receive me in your arms and make it possible for me to receive once again the divine grace. Mary, Undoer of Knots, dearest Mother, I thank you for undoing the knots in my life. Wrap me in your mantle of love, keep me under your protection, enlighten me with your peace! Amen.

IV.
GUIDE TO
CONFESSION

This Guide to Confession was prepared by Father John Trigilio

In the Sacrament of Penance, the Faithful who confess their sins to a Priest, are sorry for those sins and have a purpose of amendment, receive from God, through the absolution given by that Priest, forgiveness of sins they have committed after Baptism, and at the same time they are reconciled with the Church, which by sinning they wounded. (Canon 959)

ACT OF CONTRITION
O my God, I am heartily sorry for having offended Thee, and I detest all my sins because I dread the loss of Heaven and fear the pains of hell, but most of all, because they offend Thee, my God, who art all good and worthy of all my love. I firmly intend with the help of Thy grace to confess my sins, to do penance and to amend my life. AMEN.

EXAMINATION OF CONSCIENCE

Examine your conscience and review your sins according to the Ten Commandments, as provided below:

I. "I am the Lord, thy God, thou shalt not have strange gods before Me."

Have I sinned against Religion by seriously believing in New Age, Scientology, Astrology, Horoscopes, Fortune-telling, Superstition or engaging in the Occult? Did I endanger my Catholic Faith or cause scandal by associating with anti-Catholic groups & associations (e.g., the Freemasons)? Have fame, fortune, money, career, pleasure, etc. replaced God as my highest priority? Have I neglected my daily prayers?

II. "Thou shalt not take the name of the Lord thy God in vain."

Have I committed blasphemy by using the name of God and Jesus Christ to swear rather than to praise? Have I committed sacrilege by showing disrespect to holy objects (crucifix, rosary) or contempt for religious persons (bishop, priests, deacons, women religious) or for sacred places (in Church). Have I committed sacrilege by going to Holy Communion in the state of mortal sin without first going to confession e.g., after missing Mass on Sunday or a Holyday? Did I violate the one-hour fast before Communion? Did I break the laws of fast and abstinence during Lent? Did I neglect my Easter duty to receive Holy Communion at least once? Have I neglected to support the Church and the poor by sharing my time, talent and treasure?

III. Remember to keep holy the Sabbath day.

Did I miss Mass on any Sunday or Holyday of Obligation? (Bad weather and being sick do not count) Have I shown disrespect by leaving Mass early, not paying attention or not joining in the prayers? Did I do unnecessary work on Sunday which could have been done the day before? Have I been stingy in my support for the Church? Do I give of my time & talent?

IV. Honor thy Father and Mother.

Parents: Have I set a bad example for my children by casually missing Mass, neglecting prayer, or ignore my responsibility to provide a Catholic education by either sending my children to parochial school or to C.C.D. (Religious Education Program)? Do I show little or no interest in my children's faith and practice of it? Have I showed disrespect for those in authority, government or church? Have I not expressed my moral values to them?

Children: Have I been disobedient and/or disrespectful to my parents or guardians? Did I neglect to help them with household chores? Have I caused them unnecessary worry and anxiety by my attitude, behavior, moods, etc.?

V. Thou shalt not kill.

Did I consent, recommend, advise, approve, support or have an abortion? Did I realize that there is an excommunication for anyone who procures an abortion? Did I actively or passively cooperate with an act of euthanasia whereby ordinary means were stopped or means taken to directly end the life of an elderly or sick person? Have I committed an act of violence or abuse (physical, sexual, emotional or verbal)? Have I endangered the lives of others by reckless driving or by driving under the influence of drugs or alcohol? Do I show contempt for my body by neglecting to take care of my own health? Have I been mean or unjust to anyone? Have I held a grudge or sought revenge against someone who wronged me? Do I point out others' faults and mistakes while ignoring my own? Do I complain more than I compliment? Am I ungrateful for what other people do for me? Do I tear people down rather than encourage them? Am I prejudiced against people because of their color, language or ethnic-religious background?

VI. Thou shalt not commit adultery.

IX. Thou shalt not covet thy neighbor's wife.

Did I have any sex before or outside of marriage? Do I view pornographic material (magazines, videos, internet, hotlines)? Have I gone to massage parlors or adult book stores? Did I commit the sins of masturbation and/or artificial contraception? Have I not avoided the occasions of sin (persons or places) which would tempt me to be unfaithful to my spouse or to my own chastity? Do I encourage and entertain impure thoughts and desires? Do I tell or listen to dirty jokes? Have I committed fornication or adultery?

VII. Thou shalt not steal.

X. Thou shalt not covet thy neighbor's goods.

Have I stolen any object, committed any shoplifting or cheated anyone of their money? Did I knowingly deceive someone in business or commit fraud? Have I shown disrespect or even contempt for other people's property? Have I done any acts of vandalism? Am I greedy or envious of another's goods? Do I let financial and material concerns or the desire for comfort override my duty to God, to Church, to my family or my own spiritual well-being?

VIII. Thou shalt not bear false witness against thy neighbor.

Have I told a lie in order to deceive someone? Have I told the truth with the purpose and intention of ruining someone's reputation (sin of detraction)? Have I told a lie or spread rumors which may ruin someone's reputation (sin of calumny or slander)? Did I commit perjury by false swearing an oath on the Bible? Am I a busybody or do I love to spread gossip and secrets about others? Do I love to hear bad news about my enemies?

V.
GUIDE TO
EUCHARISTIC
ADORATION

"SOME FRUITS OF EUCHARISTIC ADORATION"

The following is a text provided by Father Michael Champagne of the Community of Jesus Crucified, who presented at the Men of Immaculata 2017 Conference.

"Can you not keep watch one hour with Me?"
Matthew 26:40, Jesus' words in the Agony in the Garden

1) **Adoration gives power!**
   a) Examples of powerful persons committed to adoration: Archbishop Fulton Sheen, St. John Paul II, St. Teresa of Calcutta

2) **Adoration gives Wisdom!**
   a) Jesus says, "Learn of Me, for I am meek and humble of heart" (Mt. 11:29)

b) Learning through divine osmosis – examples of simple people understanding profound truths

c) Pope John Paul concerning adoration: "How will young people be able to know the Lord if they are not introduced to the mystery of his Presence" (JPII, 1996).

3) Adoration Purifies and Sanctifies You!

a) Archbishop Fulton Sheen: "Adoration of the Blessed Sacrament is divine radiation"

   i) Like Moses whose face shown with the glory of the Lord as he descended from having spoken with God <u>face to face</u> (Ex. 34:29-35)

b) Catechism: "Contemplation is a gaze of faith, fixed on Jesus. 'I look at him and he looks at me': this is what a certain peasant of Ars used to say to his holy cure about his prayer before the tabernacle. This focus on Jesus is a renunciation of self. His gaze purifies our heart..." (CCC 2715).

4) Adoration gives "light for your path!"

a) Jesus said to Mother Teresa: "Come be my Light!" She lit the paths of so many because of the radiance of Jesus on her face

   i) Moses was "glowing in the dark" when He descended from Mt. Sinai after communing "face to face" with God (cf. Ex. 34:29-35).

b) "...the <u>light of the countenance of Jesus illumines the eyes of our heart and teaches us to see everything in the light of his truth and his compassion</u> for all men" (CCC 2715).

5) Adoration calms you!
  a) Divine Ritalin to combat your spiritual ADHD and ADD
  b) When prayer seems impossible, in times of grief, or anxiety – rest your head on the Bosom of Christ in Eucharistic Adoration and let the steady rhythm of His Sacred Heart bring yours into synch with Him – The Divine Pacemaker!

6) Adoration makes you patient!
  a) "Can you not watch one hour with Me?" (Mt. 26:40)
  b) "Watch and wait!" (cf. Mt. 24:42, 25:13)
  c) Adoration allows us to enter into timelessness and then we become patient with the patience of God
      i) "God's patience redeems; man's impatience crucifies" (Pope Benedict)

7) Adoration repairs the damage of sins – ours and others
  a) "Let us not refuse the time to go meet him in adoration...open to making amends for the serious offenses and crimes of the world" (CCC 1380).
  b) Even in the Tabernacle His Heart is beating with infinite love in that eternal act of redeeming the world – sitting with Him brings us into His act of redeeming and repairing

8) Adoration will convert you!
  a) *Divine cardio version!*
  b) The soldiers, having crucified Jesus, sat down and watched Him! And one of them then said, "Truly this man was Son of God!" (Mk. 15:39)

9) Adoration makes us hungry for Jesus!

a) Like St. Therese of Liseux said concerning her First Communion: "Already for a long time past, He and the little Therese had watched and understood each other."

b) Adoration is the best way to thank Jesus after receiving Him in Holy Communion and it is the best way to prepare to receive Him in our next Holy Communion

10) Adoration "tunes/sharpens" your Faith Power

a) Adoration is not popular, not only because of our lack of humility, but because of our lack of faith
   i) It takes great faith to silently, perseveringly, adore Him
   ii) But persevering, our faith power grows as it is exposed to its Divine Object – God

b) Recognizing the High Intensity Concentration, our faith is "calibrated" and becomes better able to recognize Him in others
   i) Recognizing Him in His Hidden Disguise, we become able to recognize Him in His Distressing Disguise

11) Adoration gives power to our petitions

a) "Adoration of the thrice-holy and sovereign God of love blends with humility and <u>gives assurance to our supplications</u>" (CCC 2628).

b) Notice the strict relationship between adoration and petition in the Scriptures
   i) Eliza Vaughn: 14 children, 10 vocations – 6 priests and 4 religious
   ii) Lu Monferrato, Italy – Women prayed for vocations. In 1946 323 returned

12) Adoration brings deep spiritual joy and makes you a missionary

  a) *Ite! Missa est!* "Let he who does not work, not eat!" (2 Thes. 3:10)

  b) "Let us run to our brothers and sisters and tell them, 'we've seen the Lord!'" (JPII)

  c) "Sir, we wish to see Jesus!...And they brought them to Jesus" (Jn. 12:21ff)

  d) "The disciples rejoiced to see the Risen Lord" (Jn. 20:20)

SAINT POPE JOHN PAUL II ON EUCHARISTIC ADORATION

The following is a collection of quotations from Saint Pope John Paul II regarding Eucharistic Adoration:

May we dwell long and often in adoration before Christ in the Eucharist. May we sit at **the 'school' of the Eucharist**. *From* "Letter To Priests" Signed In The Upper Room, April 20, 2000 (Holy Thusday).

I encourage Christians regularly to visit Christ present in the Blessed Sacrament, for we are all called to abide in the presence of God. In contemplation, Christians will perceive ever more profoundly the mystery at the heart of Christian life. *From* Letter to The Bishop of Liege On Feast of Corpus Christi, May 28, 1986.

We must understand that in order "to do", we must first learn "to be", that is to say, in the sweet company of Jesus in adoration.

Jesus wants you to do more than to go to Mass on Sunday. Our communal worship at Mass must go together with our personal worship of Jesus in Eucharistic adoration in order that our love may be complete ... Our essential commitment in life is to preserve and advance constantly in Eucharistic life and Eucharistic piety and to grow spiritually in the climate of the Holy Eucharist. *From Redemptor Hominis* (Redeemer Of Man), Encyclical March 4, 1979.

To contemplate the fullness of Jesus
In this silence of the white Host, carried in the Monstrance, are all His words; there is His whole life given in offering to

the Father for each of us; there is also the glory of the glorified body, which started with the Resurrection, and still continues in Heavenly union. *From* the Angelus Address at the Vatican, June 19, 1979.

When we contemplate him present in the Blessed Sacrament of the altar, Christ draws near to us and becomes more intimate to us than we are to ourselves. He grants us a share in his divine life in a transforming union and, in the Spirit, he gives us access to the Father, as he himself said to Philip: 'He who has seen me has seen the Father' (Jn. 14:9). Contemplation, which is also a Communion of desire, intimately associates us with Christ, and in a very special way associates those who are prevented from receiving it. *From* Letter to the Bishop of Liege On Feast of Corpus Christi, May 28, 1986.

For the Transformation of the World

The Church and the world have a great need of Eucharistic worship. Jesus waits for us in this sacrament of love. Let us be generous with our time in going to meet Him in adoration and in contemplation that is full of faith and ready to make reparation for the great faults and crimes of the world by our adoration never cease.... Eucharistic worship is ... the merciful and redeeming transformation of the world in the human heart. *From Dominicae Cenae* (On The Mystery And Worship Of The Eucharist), Encyclical February 24, 1980.

Closeness to Christ in silence and contemplation does not distance us from our contemporaries but, on the contrary, makes us attentive and open to human joy and distress and broadens our heart on a global scale. It unites us with our brothers and sisters in humanity and particularly with children, who are the Lord's dearly beloved.... Through adoration, the Christian mysteriously contributes to the **radical transformation of the world** and to the sowing of the Gospel. Anyone who prays to the Savior draws the gfdx whole world with him and raises it to God. Those who stand before the Lord are therefore fulfilling an eminent service. They are presenting to Christ all those who do not know him or are far from him: they keep watch in his presence on their behalf. *From* Letter to the Bishop of Liege On Feast of Corpus Christi, May 28, 1986.

For Our Personal Transformation

If we are to experience the Eucharist as the "source and summit of all Christian life" (*Lumen Gentium*, 11), then we must celebrate it with faith, receive it with reverence, and allow it to *transform our minds and hearts through the prayer of adoration.* Only by deepening our Eucharistic communion with the Lord through personal prayer can we discover what he asks of us in daily life... It is all the more important that you be *men of prayer before the Blessed Sacrament*, that you "ask God for a true spirit of adoration" ... in order to be filled with love of Christ. Only in this way can you hope to grow in the pastoral charity that makes your life and ministry fruitful. *From* Homily At Nonyong- Dong South Korea Parish, Oct. 7, 1989.

Teach young people the value of Eucharistic Adoration.

I urge priests, religious and lay people to continue and redouble their efforts to teach the younger generations the meaning and value of Eucharistic adoration and devotion. How will young people be able to know the Lord if they are not introduced to the mystery of His presence? Like the young Samuel, by learning the words of the prayer of the heart, they will be closer to the Lord, who will accompany them in their spiritual and human growth. The Eucharistic mystery is in fact the "summit of evangelization" (*Lumen Gentium*) for it is the most eminent testimony to Christ's resurrection. *From* Letter to The Bishop of Liege On Feast of Corpus Christi, May 28, 1986.

Visit the Lord in that "heart to heart" contact that is Eucharistic Adoration. Day after day, you will receive new energy to help you to bring comfort to the suffering and peace to the world. Many people are wounded by life: they are excluded from economic progress, and are without a home, a family, a job; there are people who are lost in a world of false illusions, or have abandoned all hope. By contemplating the light radiant on the face of the Risen Christ, you will learn to live as "children of the light and children of the day" (1 Th 5:5), and in this way you will show that "the fruit of light is found in all that is good and right and true" (Eph 5:9). *From* World Youth Day in Toronto, Canada, July 27, 2002.

VI.

BOOKS TO

READ

FATHER RICCARDO'S TOP 100 BOOKS

Fr. John Riccardo was ordained a priest of the Archdiocese of Detroit in 1996. He is the youngest of five children and a graduate of The University of Michigan.

After working for several years in the professional world, he entered the seminary to begin studies for the priesthood. He studied philosophy at Sacred Heart Major Seminary in Detroit, studied theology at the Gregorian University in Rome and received a Sacred License in Theology (S.T.L.) from The Pope John Paul II Institute for Studies on Marriage and the Family.

Since 2007, Fr. John has served as pastor at Our Lady of Good Counsel in Plymouth, Michigan. Prior to that, he was the pastor of St. Anastasia Catholic Church in Troy, Michigan and served at Divine Child Catholic Church in Dearborn, Michigan. He formerly served as the Director of the Cardinal Maida Institute located at St. John Center for Youth and Family in Plymouth, Michigan.

Fr. John's program, *Christ is the Answer*, focuses on catechetical teachings. He is an expert on John Paul II's Theology of the Body. He is a very popular speaker and teacher at pro-life and church events.

Fr. Riccardo has provided the following Top 100 list of books that every Catholic should read. It is not a Top 100 list, per se, because, after the first book, there is no particular order. As well, there's over a hundred books on the list.

Note that these are not all "Catholic" books in the strict sense. Not every book on this list was written by a Catholic, nor are all the books theological in nature. Take the selections from C. S. Lewis and Tolkien's *Lord of the Rings*, for example. All books, however, that are included are edifying for a Catholic.

1. The Bible (Revised Standard Version translation)
2. *The Lord* by Romano Guardini
3. *To Know Christ Jesus* by Frank Sheed
4. *The Life of Christ* by Fulton Sheen
5. *Jesus of Nazareth* by Joseph Ratzinger
6. *The Four Cardinal Virtues* by Josef Pieper
7. *What Happens at Mass* by Jeremy Driscoll
8. *Confessions* by Saint Augustine
9. *Fire of Mercy, Heart of the Word* by Erasmo Leiva Merikakis
10. *Fundamentals of the Faith* by Peter Kreeft
11. *Mere Christianity* by C.S. Lewis
12. *The Screwtape Letters* by C.S. Lewis
13. *The Essential Pope Benedict* edited by J. Thornton, S. Varenne
14. *The Theology of the Body* by Saint Pope John Paul II
15. *The Fulfillment of All Desire* by Ralph Martin
16. *A Key to the Doctrine of the Eucharist* by Abbot Vonier

17. *I Believe in Love* by D'Elbee
18. *Heart of the World* by Hans Urs von Balthasar
19. *The Birth of the Church: John: Vol. IV* by Adrienne von Speyr
20. *Crossing the Threshold of Love* by Saint Pope John Paul II
21. *Life on the Lordship of Christ* by Raniero Cantalamessa
22. *The Eucharist: Our Sanctification* by Raniero Cantalamessa
23. *On Being Catholic* by Thomas Howard
24. *By What Authority?* by Mark Shea
25. *Born Fundamentalist, Born Again Catholic* by David Currie
26. *Crossing the Tiber* by Stephen Ray
27. *The Handbook of Christian Apologetics* by Peter Kreeft & Ronald Tacelli
28. *The Lord of the Rings* by J.R.R. Tolkien
29. *The Cost of Discipleship* by Dietrich Bonhoeffer
30. *Where We Got the Bible* by Henry Graham
31. *Called to Communion* by Joseph Ratzinger
32. *The Spirit of the Liturgy* by Joseph Ratzinger
33. *The Seven Storey Mountain* by Thomas Merton
34. *The Dialogues* by Catherine of Siena
35. *The Lamb's Supper* by Scott Hahn
36. *The Handmaid of the Lord* by Adrienne von Speyr
37. *The World's First Love* by Fulton Sheen
38. *Love and Responsibility* by Saint Pope John Paul II
39. *The Splendor of Love* by Walter Schu
40. *Witness to Hope* by George Weigel
41. *The Feminist Question* by Francis Martin
42. *Healing the Original Wound* by Benedict Groeschel
43. *A Refutation of Moral Relativism* by Peter Kreeft
44. *In Search of Wisdom* by Leon Kass

45. *The Problem of Pain* by C.S. Lewis
46. *The Great Divorce* by C.S. Lewis
47. *Making Sense Out of Suffering* by Peter Kreeft
48. *God Is Near Us* by Joseph Ratzinger
49. *Confession* by Adrienne von Speyr
50. *Parochial and Plain Sermons* by Saint John Henry Newman
51. *Triumph* by David Crocker III
52. *The Evidential Power of Beauty* by Thomas Dubay
53. *Prayer* by Romano Guardini
54. *Saints for Sinners* by Alban Goodier
55. *Love's Sacred Order* by Erasmo Leiva Merikakis
56. *The Four Loves* by C.S. Lewis
57. *The Weight of Glory* by C.S. Lewis
58. *Collected Works* by Flannery O'Connor
59. *The Return of the Prodigal Son* by Henri Nouwen
60. *The Ecumenical Jihad* by Peter Kreeft
61. *The Unseriousness of Human Affairs* by Lames Schall
62. *Evangelium Vitae* by Saint Pope John Paul II
63. *Fides et Ratio* by Saint Pope John Paul II
64. *Women in the Church* edited by Louis Bouyer
65. *Catholic Bio-Ethics & the Gift of Human Life* by William E. May
66. *Marriage: The Bedrock* by William E. May
67. *The Clash of Orthodoxies* by Robert George
68. *Letters to a Young Catholic* by George Weigel
69. *Death on a Friday Afternoon* by Richard John Neuhaus
70. *Why Humanae Vitae Was Right* edited by Janet Smith
71. *20th Century Martyrs* by Robert Royal
72. *Testimony to Hope* by Xavier Nguyen
73. *The Divine Comedy* by Dante (Sayers translation)

74. *Arise From This Darkness* by Benedict Groeschel
75. *Orthodoxy* by G.K. Chesterton
76. *Thomas Aquinas* by G.K. Chesterton
77. *Saint Francis* by G.K. Chesterton
78. *Edmund Campion* by Evelyn Waugh
79. *Brideshead Revisited* by Evelyn Waugh
80. *A Simple Path* by Saint Teresa of Calcutta
81. *The Rise of Christianity* by Rodney Stark
82. *Manual of Prayers* by Joseph T. McGloin
83. *Fire Within* by Thomas Dubay
84. *Architects of the Culture of Death* by Donald De-marco & B. Wiker
85. *Transformation in Christ* by Dietrich von Hilde-brand
86. *The Hidden Manna* by James O'Connor
87. *Introduction to the Devout Life* by Saint Francis De Sales
88. *Perelandra* (Book One of *The Space Trilogy*) by C.S. Lewis
89. *The Chronicles of Narnia* by C.S. Lewis
90. *Back to Virtue* by Peter Kreeft
91. *The Crisis of Islam* by Bernard Lewis
92. *What Went Wrong?* by Bernard Lewis
93. *The Bible and the Quran* by Jacques Jomier
94. *What Difference Does Jesus Make?* by Frank Sheed
95. *Coming Soon* by Michael Barber
96. *The Resurrection of the Son of God* by N.T. Wright
97. *Eucharistic Presence: A Study ...* by Robert Sokolowski
98. *The Diary of Divine Mercy* St. Faustina
99. *Catholicism: The Common Destiny of Man* by Henri De Lubac
100. *The Drama of Atheistic Humanism* by Henri De Lubac

101. *Strong Fathers, Strong Daughters* by Meg Meeker
102. *How Now Shall We Live?* by Charles Colson & Nancy Pearcey
103. *That Man Is You* by Louis Evely
104. *Loving the Church* by Christoph Schonborn
105. *The Power of the Cross* by Raniero Cantalamessa

ADDITIONS TO THE TOP 100 BY THE MEN OF THE IMMACULATA

1. *Ignatius Catholic Study Bible* from Ignatius Press
2. *The Weight of a Mass: A Tale of Faith* by Josephine Nobisso
3. *Father Elijah: An Apocalypse* by Michael O'Brien
4. *A Landscape With Dragons* by Michael O'Brien
5. *The Everlasting Man* by G. K. Chesterton
6. *A Man For All Seasons* by Robert Bolt
7. *Jesus and the Jewish Roots of the Eucharist* by Brant Pitre
8. *The Case for Christ* by Brant Pitre
9. *Hail, Holy Queen* by Scott Hahn
10. *A Father Who Keeps His Promises* by Scott Hahn
11. *Les Miserables* by Victor Hugo
12. *Behold the Man* by Deacon Harold Burke-Sivers
13. *Unplanned* by Abby Johnson
14. *The Princess Kiss* by Jennie Bishop
15. *The Squire and the Scroll* by Jennie Bishop
16. *Kristin Lavransdatter* by Sigrid Undset

VII.

HYMNS

O Salutaris Hostia (O Saving Victim)

O Salutaris Hostia is from the last two verses of Verbum Supernum, one of the five Eucharistic Hymns written by St. Thomas Aquinas (1225-1274) at the request of Pope Urban IV (1261-1264) when the Pope first instituted the Feast of Corpus Christi in 1264. The prayer is still used today, often at exposition of the Blessed Sacrament.

O saving Victim,
Open wide the gate of heaven to us below.
Our foes press on from every side;
Your aid supply, your strength bestow.
To your great name be endless praise,
Immortal Godhead, One in Three;
O grant us endless length of days
In our true native land with thee. Amen.

O salutaris Hostia
Quae caeli pandis ostium;
Bella premunt hostilia,
Da robur, fer auxillium.
Uni trinoque Domino
Sit sempiterna gloria,
Qui vitam sine termino
Nobis donet in patria.
Amen.

Tantum Ergo (Down in Adoration Falling)

Tantum Ergo is the last two stanzas from the Eucharistic Hymn (Pange Lingua) composed by St. Thomas Aquinas and is used at Benediction of the Blessed Sacrament. The response and the prayer at the end is a later addition used at Benediction. A partial indulgence is granted to the faithful who recite it and a plenary indulgence is granted to those who recite it on Holy Thursday or Corpus Christi.

Down in adoration falling,
This great Sacrament we hail;
Over ancient forms of worship
Newer rites of grace prevail;
Faith will tell us Christ is present,
When our human senses fail.

Tantum ergo Sacramentum
Veneremur cernui,
Et antiquum documentum
Novo cedat ritui;
Praestet fides supplementum
Sensuum defectfui.

To the everlasting Father,
And the Son who made us free,
And the Spirit, God proceeding
From them Each eternally,
Be salvation, honor, blessing,
Might and endless majesty.
Amen.

Genitori Gentioque
Laus et jubilatio,
Salus, honor, virtus quoque
Sit et benedictio;
Procedenti ab utroque
Compar sit laudatio. Amen.

Priest/Deacon: You have given them Bread from heaven
ALL: Having all sweetness within it.
Priest/Deacon: Let us pray: O God, who in this wonderful Sacrament left us a memorial of Thy Passion: grant, we implore Thee, that we may so venerate the sacred mysteries of Thy Body and Blood, as always to be conscious of the fruit of Thy Redemption. Thou who livest and reignest forever and ever.
ALL: Amen.

VENI, VENI EMMANUEL (O COME, O COME, EMMANUEL)

Veni, Veni Emmanuel is a synthesis of the great "O Antiphons" that are used for Vespers during the octave before Christmas (Dec. 17-23). These antiphons are of ancient origin, dating back to at least the ninth century. The hymn itself, though, is much more recent. Its first appeared in the 18th century in the Psalteriolum Cantionum Catholicarum (Cologne 1710).

There are several arrangements of this hymn. The one below gives the seven verses in the order in which the antiphons appear during the octave before Christmas, except for the first verse, which really is the last of the O antiphons and would otherwise go at the end if it were not the standard first verse of the hymn. It is interesting to note that the initial words of the actual antiphons in reverse order form the acrostic ERO CRAS, which can be loosely translated as "I will be there tomorrow": O Emmanuel, O Rex, O Oriens, O Clavis, O Radix ("virgula" in the hymn), O Adonai, O Sapientia. That is a fitting message indeed since Christ's birth falls on the following day.

Veni veni, Emmanuel captivum solve Israel, qui gemit in exsilio, privatus Dei Filio. R: Gaude! Gaude! Emmanuel, nascetur pro te Israel!	O come, O come, Emmanuel, and ransom captive Israel, that morns in lonely exile here until the Son of God appear. R: Rejoice! Rejoice! O Israel, to thee shall come Emmanuel!
Veni, O Sapientia, quae hic disponis omnia, veni, viam prudentiae ut doceas et gloriae. **R.**	O come, Thou Wisdom, from on high, and order all things far and nigh; to us the path of knowledge show, and teach us in her ways to go. **R.**

Veni, veni, Adonai,
qui populo in Sinai
legem dedisti vertice
in maiestate gloriae. **R.**

O come, o come, Thou Lord of
might,
who to thy tribes on Sinai's height
in ancient times did give the law,
in cloud, and majesty, and awe. **R.**

Veni, O Iesse virgula,
ex hostis tuos ungula,
de spectu tuos tartari
educ et antro bar-
athri. **R.**

O come, Thou Rod of Jesse's stem,
from ev'ry foe deliver them
that trust Thy mighty power to save,
and give them vict'ry o'er the
grave. **R.**

Veni, Clavis Davidica,
regna reclude caelica,
fac iter tutum superum,
et claude vias infer-
um. **R.**

O come, Thou Key of David, come,
and open wide our heav'nly home,
make safe the way that leads on high,
that we no more have cause to sigh. **R.**

Veni, veni O Oriens,
solare nos adveniens,
noctis depelle nebulas,
dirasque mortis tene-
bras. **R.**

O come, Thou Dayspring from on
high,
and cheer us by thy drawing nigh;
disperse the gloomy clouds of night
and death's dark shadow put to
flight. **R.**

Veni, veni, Rex Genti-
um,
veni, Redemptor omni-
um,
ut salvas tuos famulos
peccati sibi conscios. **R.**

O come, Desire of the nations, bind
in one the hearts of all mankind;
bid every strife and quarrel cease
and fill the world with heaven's
peace. **R.**

Salve Regina (Hail, Holy Queen)

Hail, Holy Queen enthroned above, O Maria.
Hail, Queen of mercy and of love, O Maria.
Triumph, all ye cherubim, Sing with us, ye seraphim,
Heaven and earth resound the hymn:
Salve, salve, salve Regina!

Our life, our sweetness, here below, O Maria!
Our hope in sorrow and in woe, O Maria!
Triumph, all ye cherubim, Sing with us, ye seraphim,
Heaven and earth resound the hymn:
Salve, salve, salve Regina!

To thee we cry, poor sons of Eve, O Maria!
To thee we sigh, we mourn, we grieve, O Maria!
Triumph, all ye cherubim, Sing with us, ye seraphim,
Heaven and earth resound the hymn:
Salve, salve, salve Regina!

Turn then most gracious Advocate, O Maria!
Toward us thine eyes compassionate, O Maria!
Triumph, all ye cherubim, Sing with us, ye seraphim,
Heaven and earth resound the hymn:
Salve, salve, salve Regina!

The cause of joy to men below, O Maria!
The spring through which all graces flow, O Maria!

Angels, all your praises bring, Earth and heaven, with us sing,
All creation echoing: Salve, salve, salve Regina!

AMAZING GRACE

Amazing grace! How sweet the sound
That saved a wretch like me!
I once was lost, but now am found;
Was blind, but now I see.

'Twas grace that taught my heart to fear,
And grace my fears relieved;
How precious did that grace appear
The hour I first believed.

Through many dangers, toils and snares,
I have already come;
'Tis grace hath brought me safe thus far,
And grace will lead me home.

The Lord has promised good to me,
His word my hope secures;
He will my shield and portion be,
As long as life endures.

Yea, when this flesh and heart shall fail,
And mortal life shall cease,
I shall possess, within the veil,
A life of joy and peace.

The world shall soon dissolve like snow,
The sun refuse to shine;
But God, who called me here below,
Shall be forever mine.

When we've been there ten thousand years,
Bright shining as the sun,
We've no less days to sing God's praise
Than when we'd first begun.

HERE I AM, LORD

I, the Lord of sea and sky,
I have heard My people cry.
All who dwell in dark and sin,
My hand will save.
I who made the stars of night,
I will make their darkness bright.
Who will bear My light to them?
Whom shall I send?

Here I am Lord, Is it I, Lord?
I have heard You calling in the night.
I will go Lord, if You lead me.
I will hold Your people in my heart.

I, the Lord of snow and rain,
I have borne my people's pain.
I have wept for love of them, They turn away.
I will break their hearts of stone,
Give them hearts for love alone.
I will speak My word to them
Whom shall I send?

Here I am Lord, Is it I, Lord?
I have heard You calling in the night.
I will go Lord, if You lead me.
I will hold Your people in my heart.

I, the Lord of wind and flame
I will tend the poor and lame.
I will set a feast for them,
My hand will save

Finest bread I will provide,
Till their hearts be satisfied.
I will give My life to them,
Whom shall I send?

Here I am Lord, Is it I, Lord?
I have heard You calling in the night.
I will go Lord, if You lead me.
I will hold Your people in my heart.

VIII.

LITURGICAL

CALENDAR

January
1 — **THE SOLEMNITY OF MARY, MOTHER OF GOD**
4 — Saint Elizabeth Ann Seton[†]
5 — Saint John Neumann[†]
6 — Saint André Bessette[†]
22 — Day of Prayer, Legal Protection of Unborn Children; 23
if 22 falls on a Sunday
23 — Saint Vincent, Deacon and Martyr; Saint Marianne
Cope, Virgin[†]
25 — Conversion of St. Paul

February
2 — Purification of the Blessed Virgin Mary (also called Can-
dlemas)
3 — Saint Blaise (blessing of throats)
14 — Saint Valentine

March
3 — Saint Katharine Drexel, Virgin[†]
99

8 — Saint Thomas Aquinas
17 — Saint Patrick
19 — Saint Joseph, Foster Father of Our Lord
25 — Annunciation of the Blessed Virgin Mary

Easter Liturgies

Quinquagesima Sunday	Easter minus 50 days; Sunday before Ash Wednesday
Mardi Gras	Tuesday before Ash Wednesday (no prescribed liturgy)
Ash Wednesday	Easter minus 46 days; Wednesday before First Sunday of Lent
Laetare Sunday	Fourth Sunday of Lent; "Rejoice (Laetare), Jerusalem" (Is 66:10-11)
Palm Sunday	Sunday before Easter; Sixth Sunday of Lent
Holy Thursday	Thursday before Easter
Good Friday	Friday before Easter
Easter	First Sunday after the "Paschal" full moon, which is the first full moon on or after March 21
Octave of Easter	Eight days of feasting; Easter Sunday to Divine Mercy Sunday
Divine Mercy	First Sunday after Easter
ASCENSION	Thursday of the Sixth Week of Easter; 40th day of Easter
Pentecost	50th day of Easter (49th after Easter); Seventh Sunday of Easter
Trinity Sunday	Sunday after Pentecost; Solemnity
Corpus Christi	2nd Sunday after Pentecost; Most Holy Body and Blood of Christ
Sacred Heart	19th day after Pentecost

May

1 — Saint Joseph the Worker

10 — Saint Damien of Molokai, Priest[+]

13 — Our Lady of Fatima

15 — Saint Isidore the Farmer

June

13 — Saint Anthony of Padua

29 — Saints Peter and Paul

July

1 — Saint Junípero Serra, Priest[+]

2 — Feast of the Visitation of St. Elizabeth by the B.V.M.

4 — Independence Day

14 — Saint Kateri Tekakwitha, Virgin[+]

19 — Saint Vincent de Paul

22 — Saint Mary Magdalene

26 — Saint Anne, Mother of the B.V.M.

August

6 — Transfiguration of Our Lord

9 — St. Edith Stein (St. Teresa Benedicta of the Cross)

14 — Saint Maximilian Kolbe

15 — **THE ASSUMPTION OF THE B.V.M. (SOLEM-NITY)**

28 — Saint Augustine

30 — Saint Rose of Lima

September

5 — Saint Teresa of Calcutta

9 — Saint Peter Claver, Priest

23 — St. (Padre) Pio, Stigmatic, Confessor

October

1 — Saint Thérèse of Lisieux

4 — Saint Francis of Assisi

5 — Blessed Francis Xavier Seelos, Priest[†]

19 — Saints John de Brébeuf and Isaac Jogues and Companions, Martyrs[†]

20 — Saint Paul of the Cross, Priest

22 — Pope Saint John Paul the Great

28 — St. Jude Thaddaeus, patron of hopeless causes

Christ the King — last Sunday of October; Sunday before All Saints

November

1 — **ALL SAINTS DAY (SOLEMNITY)**

2 — All Souls Day

3 — Saint Martin de Porres

13 — Saint Frances Xavier Cabrini, Virgin[†]

18 — Saint Rose Philippine Duchesne, Virgin[†]

23 — Blessed Miguel Agustín Pro, Priest and Martyr[†]

Fourth Thursday — Thanksgiving Day

December

6 — Saint Nicholas

8 — **IMMACULATE CONCEPTION OF THE B.V.M. (SOLEMNITY)**; Patronal feast day of the United States of America

12 — Our Lady of Guadalupe

13 — Saint Lucy, Virgin Martyr

25 — **CHRISTMAS (SOLEMNITY)**

26 — Saint Stephen the First Martyr

27 — Saint John the Apostle

Christmas Liturgies

1st Sun. of Advent	Sunday nearest to feast of St. Andrew the Apostle (Nov. 30); Sunday between Nov. 27 and Dec. 3
Gaudete Sunday	Third Sunday of Advent
CHRISTMAS	December 25
Epiphany	Sunday between January 2 and 8
Baptism of Jesus	Sunday after Epiphany –or– on the octave of the Epiphany

KEY:

ALL CAPS, BOLD TYPE — Holy Days of Obligation per Canon 1246, §2, in addition to Sunday. Note: Whenever January 1, the solemnity of Mary, Mother of God, or August 15, the solemnity of the Assumption, or November 1, the solemnity of All Saints, falls on a Saturday or on a Monday, the precept to attend Mass is abrogated.

† — North American Saint or Blessed

IX.

APPS, BLOGS, & WEBSITES

TOP FIVE CATHOLIC APPS

1. Laudate [FREE]

If you have room for just one app, this is the one. It has most everything: Daily Readings, Saint of the Day, Liturgy of the Hours, Order of the Mass, Rosary and Chaplets, Examination of Conscience for Confession, and all your other Catholic Prayers. It's almost as good as this book! Basically all the other apps in this list are contained within this one, except for a translation of the Holy Bible, which VerseWise (below) give you.

2. iBreviary [FREE]

From FOCUS (Fellowship of Catholic University Students): "[O]n top of eliminating the need to carry your breviary around with you all the time, it also cues up the prayers for the day, eliminating the need to coordinate ribbons and flip back and forth in a book."

3. VerseWise [PAID]

Best Bible App! The Revised Standard Version – Catholic Edition (RSV-CE) is highly recommended. This particular

Bible translation is the closest to the original text, and it shines in this app. It's highly searchable, copy-and-pastable, and well-organized.

"Truth & Life" is another good Scripture app.

4. The Confession App [PAID]

From CatholicApptitude.org: "Interactive features of this app help engage you in the process of making a good confession from examination of conscience to absolution. If you are new to the sacrament or have forgotten how to make a good confession, this app provides gentle and encouraging help every step of the way. It is designed to make the process easy for you by providing a comprehensive examination of conscience with large check boxes for items you wish to confess. Your choices (and any text you type in) get distilled into a separate Confession Guide for you to take into the confessional to walk you through everything you need to say including your Act of Contrition. Large font makes it easy to read in the low light setting. Feel secure knowing no data is stored to the phone hard drive or to the internet. The really cool part? After confession, you get the satisfaction of being able to hit the "Erase My Sins" button and watch your check marked sins removed from the temporary cache in the phone or tablet—a technological symbol of what just happened to your soul!"

5. Covenant Eyes [PAID: subscription fees]

This is an app to help shield yourself from the scourge of pornography. Here's a description from its maker: "This app is an Internet browser for users of Covenant Eyes Accountability and Filtering. It is designed to replace Safari. If you use Accountability, sites that you visit using this browser are monitored and reported on your Accountability Report. If you also use the Covenant Eyes Filter, sites will be blocked based on your Filter Sensitivity Level and your custom block/allow list."

Honorable Mentions: (1) iPieta [PAID] which has an amazing library of Catholic resources and spiritual writings;

(2) Catholic Mega App [FREE]; (3) Catholic Church App [FREE]

TOP TEN CATHOLIC WEBSITES

1. Catholic Answers (www.catholic.com)
All the best Catholic apologists contribute to this website, as well as the Catholic Answers Live call-in radio show, including Jimmy Akin, Trent Horn, Louisianan Karlo Broussard, Jim Blackburn, Tim Staples, Karl Keating, and Patrick Madrid. The Forums are also a great place to ask questions and join discussions.

2. The Vatican Website (w2.vatican.va/content/vatican/en.html)
The Vatican's website is extraordinary, as it should be. It has pretty much everything that was ever issued from the Vatican – you can filter "by century." It has basically all the writings of all the popes, from encyclicals to speeches, plus lots of video. Just like the Church, herself, it's both a truly massive database of Catholic thought or just a good place to stop by daily.

3. The USCCB (United States Conference of Catholic Bishops) Website (http://www.usccb.org/)
Similar to the Vatican's website, this site can be both a useful resource and database or just a good place for the daily happenings of the Church in America.

4. Life News (www.lifenews.com)
This site and the next site are tied for the best Pro-Life New source. LifeNews is not to be confused with LifeSiteNews.

From the site: "LifeNews.com is an independent news agency devoted to reporting news that affects the pro-life community. With a team of experienced journalists and bloggers, LifeNews.com reaches more than 750,000 pro-life advocates each week via our web site, email news reports, social networking outreach and weekday radio program. LifeNews.com also acts as a service provider to furnish news content to media that share the pro-life perspective. The topics covered by LifeNews.com include abortion, assisted suicide and euthanasia, bioethics issues such as human cloning and stem cell research, campaigns and elections, and cultural legal and legislative issues as they affect the pro-life community."

5. Live Action (liveaction.org)

From the site: "Live Action News reports daily on stories the mainstream media often refuses to cover — including exposés of the abortion industry and stories revealing the dignity and humanity of preborn children — inspiring our readers to defend the most vulnerable within their communities."

6. National Catholic Register (www.ncregister.com)

Not to be confused with the *National Catholic Reporter*, which might be mistaken for a Catholic news source, the *Register* is a service of EWTN. This is a good place to verify news stories that the Mainstream Media might be contorting or misreporting.

7. New Advent Catholic Encyclopedia (newadvent.org)

Very thorough Catholic Encyclopedia – this has been the gold standard for the last century or so. You may still find the multi-multi-volume print edition on the shelves of libraries, public or private. It even has its own blog or newsfeed, similar to a Catholic Drudge Report.

8. EWTNews (www.ewtn.com)

Your #1 Catholic news and programming source – so good it's basically included twice, if you count the *National Catholic Register*.

9. The American Catholic (the-american-catholic.com)

From the site: *"The American Catholic* is an online community of Christians, motivated by a rich heritage of Catholic spiritual and intellectual tradition, seeking to engage American society and culture in pursuit of the common good. Following the Second Vatican Council's ecclesial call for greater Christian witness in contemporary society, we are dedicated to the renewal and "Christian animation of the temporal order." We are all deeply inspired by our Catholic faith and seek authentic sacramental lives centered upon the "broken bread" of the Eucharist, the source and summit of the Christian life."

10. The Catholic Company (www.catholiccompany.com)

I thought I ought to include at least one Catholic online gift store. This is the World's #1 Catholic store, according to the website, and I believe it. This is a great place to stock up on Catholic items or buy gifts for Baptisms, First Communions, Confirmation, etc.

Honorable Mentions:

- Dr. Brant Pitre's website (www.BrantPitre.com) includes his Bible studies on CD, DVD, MP3 visit
- The St. Paul Center for Biblical Theology (stpaul-center.com) also has a tremendous amount of resources, including online courses, from Dr. Scott Hahn, as well as Dr. Pitre and others.
- Sister John Thomas recommends the following:
  - Angelic Warfare Confraternity (www.angelic-warfareconfraternity.org) which also includes a blog and "Prayers for Purity" which have been included in the "Important Prayers & Novenas" chapter;
  - Celebrate Calm (www.celebratecalm.com): per Sister John Thomas, "This speaker has been very effective with our dads and has a great CD called 'Straight Talk for Dads'"

Top Ten (+1) Catholic Blogs

The following is loose ranking of the top Catholic blogs, cobbled together from other rankings and which are intended to span the range of Catholic thinking and topics.

1. **The Catholic Gentleman
   (www.catholicgentleman.net)**
   "More than ever, the Church needs men. Sadly, many Catholic men have believed the lie that being holy isn't manly, and that the faith is boring. They leave religion to women and children and simply tune out. But holiness is for men. There is nothing more difficult, rewarding, or manly than becoming a saint. [...] The Catholic Gentleman exists to inspire men to holiness—to love God, to serve others, and to deny self. And to do it all with class and classic manly flair."

2. **Catholic Vote Blog
   (www.catholicvote.org/blog)**
   Catholic Vote is a prominent voice in conservative politics, and their blog hosts several authors, including Thomas Peters, the self-styled "American Papist."

3. **Dr. Taylor Marshall
   (www.taylormarshall.com)**
   Former Episcopalian priest who was received into the Catholic Church. His conversion has been featured on EWTN's *Journey Home* withe Marcus Grodi (twice). He describes himself, theologically, as a "rock-ribbed Thomist."

4. **Fr. Z's Blog (wdtprs.com/blog/) by Fr. John Zuhlsdorf**
   "This blog is rather like a fusion of the Baroque 'salon' with its well-tuned harpsichord around which polite society gathered for entertainment and edification and, on the other hand, a Wild West "saloon" with its out-of-tune piano and swinging doors, where everyone has a gun and something to say. Nevertheless, we try to point our discussions back to what it is to be Catholic in this increasingly difficult age, to love God, and how to get to heaven."

5. **Cardinal Dolan's Blog**

(www.cardinaldolan.org)

The official blog of the Prince of NYC, His Eminence, Timothy Cardinal Dolan – the site also includes the Cardinal's homilies and podcasts.

6. The Catholic Thing
(www.thecatholicthing.org)

From the inaugural post by Editor-in-Chief Robert Royal: "Wide-ranging and solid Catholic commentary on events is necessary, not only to keep us from being overwhelmed by the tsunami of information now coming at us all from many sources, but to cast a steady and invigorating Catholic light on what is otherwise a superficial and dull world."

7. Dominicana
(www.dominicanajournal.org)

"Dominicana is a publication of the Dominican student brothers of the St. Joseph Province of the Order of Preachers. We live and study at the Dominican House of Studies and at St. Dominic's Priory, both in Washington, D.C. Our lives are given over to prayer, the intellectual life, and preaching. Blog posts are updated every weekday, and the journal appears twice a year."

8. The Curt Jester Blog
(www.splendoroftruth.com/curtjester)

From the blog: "Jeff Miller is a former atheist who after spending forty years in the wilderness finds himself with both astonishment and joy a member of the Catholic Church. This award winning blog presents my hopefully humorous and sometimes serious take on things religious, political, and whatever else crosses my mind."

9. Fr. Dwight Longenecker
(www.dwightlongenecker.com)

"I'm a former Evangelical, then an Anglican priest, now a Catholic priest." He graduated from the Christian Fundamentalist Bob Jones University and went on to study theology at Oxford Univeristy – a radical change. He blogs mainly on liturgical catechesis and commentary, but his range extends to *The Lord of the Rings* and the possibility of aliens, as well.

10. Those Catholic Men
(www. thosecatholicmen.com)

"Three years ago, a fraternity from Indiana set out to address an unspoken reality in the Catholic Church: the disconnect between the Church and Her men. This website is an online resource for Catholic men amidst the confusion of our post-Christian, secular age. We believe that Catholic men must make preparations for the struggles to come by prayer, asceticism, study and brotherhood. In these times, we need men who think with converted minds, desire with converted hearts, and feel with converted affections. Status quo Catholicism will not hold. Our church, country, parishes, wives, sons and daughters are counting on us. There's a world to win for Christ the King. From our fraternity to yours: do not underestimate your power as a man to witness to the saving truth of Jesus Christ."

11. Scott Smith "All Roads Lead to Rome"
(www.thescottsmithblog.com)

SELF-PROMOTION WARNING: This is the blog of the main author/editor of this book and co-founder of the Men of the Immaculata, Scott Smith. It didn't feel right putting my own blog in the Top 10, so I put it in the *Top 11*. I blog on wide-ranging topics including Catholic Apologetics, Theology in the Movies, and Pro-Life topics.

Honorable Mentions:

Whispers in the Loggia (whispersintheloggia.blogspot.com); American Papist by Thomas Peters (www.american-papist.com), Peters would have his own spot but he's a contributor to the Catholic Vote blog; and

Rorate Caeli (rorate-caeli.blogspot.com).

X.

ABORTION &
FATHERHOOD:
MEN SUFFER TOO

Nearly 61 million abortions have taken place in our country since abortion was legalized in 1973. Given these startling numbers, we immediately recognize the enormity of the tragic loss of innocent human life.

What these numbers do not reflect, however, is the way that abortion impacts more than the woman who has the abortion. Abortion affects families, relatives, friends, co-workers and, ultimately, all of us. The people that are often overlooked by society as being greatly impacted by abortion are the fathers.

While it can be very difficult for women to seek healing and forgiveness after an abortion, it is perhaps even more difficult for some men because of the way that fathers are marginalized in discussions about abortion. The reality is that men also suffer as a result of abortion.

BEFORE THE ABORTION

Prior to the abortion, men may feel as though they don't have a "right" to encourage the woman to not abort. The father may be left out of the decision completely, leaving him feeling powerless. The experience that this man shares is not uncommon.

In October of 2006 I found out I was going to be a Father. My girlfriend of 6 months was pregnant with our child. Neither of us planned this pregnancy, or had even talked about the possibility of getting pregnant. That was about to become my biggest regret. Like I said I wasn't ready to have a child. She said she couldn't go forth in having a child and needed to abort... Her sister had offered to pay $500 for her to get an abortion. She insisted she was going to get the abortion, was planning to get one that weekend, and broke up with me right before.

I called the abortion clinic and asked what my rights were; they said "You don't have any". I then asked them, "What do you do with the aborted babies? I want to bury my child." They told me that it wasn't a child, it was a fetus, and to never call again or they would involve the police. My hands were tied. I, as a father had no legal right to protect my child from a death committed by a "doctor". I called everyone imaginable to see what my rights were and I got the same answer: "nothing".

The week before my child was aborted; I went to try one more time to ask the mother of my child to not do this. But she was adamant about having an abortion,

and told me to leave. So I then asked her if I could do one thing before I left, she told me that was fine. I then got on my knees and kissed the stomach of the mother of my child and said "I love you, and Daddy will see you in heaven." I then took the ultrasound pictures and left.
- Theo (Lumina Ministry, www.postabortionhelp.com. Used with permission.)

In other cases, men may encourage and do everything in their power to make sure the abortion happens. The realization of the life lost and his role in that may remain suppressed for years. The subconscious may do everything in its power to keep it suppressed. For others, the realization is immediate, though it may be repressed in an effort to "get back to normal." Ivan remembers the events leading up to the abortion of his child.

We had started to go out recently, less than a month, when we became sexually active. Before two months had gone by, she suspected she was pregnant. She wasn't in a good moment in her life. Many hard situations in her past had brought their toll on her, including an instance of sexual abuse, extreme poverty and other types of really cruel, emotional abuse. I was attracted to her a lot, but we weren't in love, everything was too new for love to have grown.

At that time I didn't want to have a kid with her, as I thought strongly it didn't fit my plans. My plans weren't bad plans by the way, they were plans for a stable family upbringing. When I heard she was pregnant, I got desperate.

I felt that heavy burden of having an unplanned baby with someone I didn't really know and trust would be too much. It was so far away from what I thought I could handle. I had so many plans as well. I thought that, for example, traveling the world as I wished would be impossible. I wouldn't be able to go out anymore as I liked, having fun as a single guy. I wouldn't have the possibility to feel the "joy" of being a "free spirit" in NYC anymore, one without strings attached. I didn't want to have a baby with someone that wasn't in love with me and I wasn't in love with them, I didn't want to go through the scary instability this would bring. I had a responsible father, so I wanted to be one as well, so I didn't want to go through with having a kid that I wouldn't know if I could be really present for him.

...I don't remember thinking at all of a creature in her womb whom whose father I was, so, I told her to abort. She didn't want to at first, but I helped talk her into it. I was insistent, mostly through my own victimization.

...The moment I heard from her, "IT WAS DONE," I knew something terrible had happened. I felt cold and desperate inside. I became so sorry. Sorry to her, sorry for what could have been, sorry to God, the one who Created me and that little creature in her womb, He that gives us this life, this miracle of Life.

- Ivan (Lumina Ministry, www.postabortionhelp.com. Used with permission.)

AFTER THE ABORTION

Whatever the circumstances surrounding the abortion, the emotions and suffering that men experience is real and needs to be acknowledged. Unfortunately, we often discuss post-abortion grief and healing in a way that excludes men, leading to an increased sense of isolation. Some common reactions that fathers may experience, which they may or may not connect to the abortion, include:

- **Anger or rage**
  Anger may be directed at oneself for the role played in the abortion taking place or towards others that encouraged or forced the abortion. This anger may be internalized (linked to communication difficulties and depression) or externalized (shouting, disrespecting others, name-calling, criticism). Anger or rage may also lead to an impulse to lash out physically at others.

- **A wounded sense of masculinity**
  It is natural for men to feel responsible for those they love. Part of that responsibility is protecting the ones they love from harm. After an abortion, a man may feel that he was not able to protect his partner or offspring.

- **Inability to communicate with partner**
  Communication may break down after an abortion. Women and men respond to grief differently. Phrases such as, "Why don't you just get over it?" may be used. These phrases are not productive and tend to increase conflict.

- **Alcohol or drug abuse**
  This tends to be a common coping mechanism shared by men. Some men will seek treatment through AA, NA or some other program. However, if the issue of abortion is not raised, treatment may be impaired.

- **Grief and sadness**
  The grief and sadness may surprise men. It can be difficult for men to articulate feelings of grief or sadness. There may be few friends that men feel comfortable enough with to share these feelings.

- **Risk taking behaviors**
  Frustration and anger associated with unresolved grief may result in behaviors such as driving fast, sky-diving,

or other death-defying acts. Men who opposed the abortion may verge on being suicidal.

HEALING AND FORGIVENESS

Healing and forgiveness are possible. God, who is Love and Mercy, is calling fathers to seek His help and forgiveness. Some may believe that they can't be forgiven or even shouldn't be forgiven. Know that there is no sin that God cannot forgive, including the sin of abortion. Forgiveness is not about us or the magnitude of our sin. Forgiveness is about the infinite love and mercy of God!

Having the sin of abortion forgiven does not mean that the healing is done. Healing from abortion is often a long process involving mourning the loss of the child, working through the multitude of feelings which may include guilt, anger and lack of self-forgiveness, growing in deeper relationship with God and more. This all requires time and patience.

While the process of healing may be difficult, Pope Saint John Paul II offers these words of hope:

The Church is aware of the many factors which may have influenced your decision, and she does not doubt that in many cases it was a painful and even shattering decision. The wound in your heart may not yet have healed. Certainly what happened was and remains terribly wrong. But do not give in to discouragement and do not lose hope. Try rather to understand what happened and face it honestly. If you have not already done so, give yourselves over with humility and trust to repentance. The Father of mercies is ready to give you his forgiveness and his peace in the Sacrament of Reconciliation. To the same Father and his mercy you can with sure hope entrust your child. With the friendly and ex-

pert help and advice of other people, and as a result of your own painful experience, you can be among the most eloquent defenders of everyone's right to life. Through your commitment to life, whether by accepting the birth of other children or by welcoming and caring for those most in need of someone to be close to them, you will become promoters of a new way of looking at human life. (EV 99)

Resources

The path to healing and forgiveness does not have to be travelled alone. Whether the father is setting out on the journey or has already begun the healing process, there are trained individuals and resources available to help. There is hope after abortion.

Entering Canaan - Baton Rouge
Retreats, Monthly Gatherings
(every other month, spiritual focus)
www.EnteringCanaan.com
256-568-6004
Email: EnteringCanaanBR@diobr.org

Woman's New Life Center
Post-abortion counseling for *both* men and women
Baton Rouge: 225-663-6470
New Orleans: 504-831-3117
www.womansnewlife.com

Catholic Charities Post-Abortion Counseling
225-267-4673
Email: ProjectRachel@ccdiobr.org

Reclaiming Fatherhood - A Multifaceted Examination of Men Dealing with Abortion

www.MenandAbortion.info

Rachel's Vineyard

www.RachelsVineyard.org

Weekend retreats for men and women who have experienced abortion.

To get involved in the pro-life movement in Louisiana:

Louisiana Right to Life

Ben Clapper, Executive Director
www.prolifelouisiana.org
Email: info@prolifelouisiana.org
Toll Free Phone: 866.463.5433

New Orleans

Address: 200 Robert E. Lee Blvd., New Orleans, LA 70124
Local Phone: 504.835.6520

Lafayette

Mailing Address: P.O. Box 5247, Lafayette, LA 70502
Physical Address: 600 Jefferson St. Suite 506, Lafayette, LA 70501
Local Phone: 337.524.0044

XI.

MARIAN

CONSECRATION

"The Immaculate alone has from God the promise of victory over Satan. She seeks souls that will consecrate themselves entirely to her, that will become in her hands forceful instruments for the defeat of Satan and the spread of God's kingdom."
- St. Maximilian Kolbe

Not long before becoming pope, Pope Francis urged the world to look towards Mary and the Holy Family for defense and protection, and to do so fervently. He promoted St. John Bosco's famous dream: devotion to Mary, along with the Eucharist, are the immovable anchors that will guide the Church on the path to heaven. Pope Francis has said "The Eucharist has been given to us so that our life, like that of Mary, can completely become a Magnificat."

OVERVIEW OF THE MARIAN CONSECRATION

You made a Preliminary Act of Consecration at the Men of the Immaculata Catholic Men's Conference on March 9, 2019, the first Saturday of Lent. Now, you will prepare for your final consecration as you journey through the rest of Lent alongside Jesus and Mary.

The next 33 days of prayers and readings are the preparation for your Act of Consecration. The 34th day will be your day of consecration.

St. Louis de Montfort divides the 33 days into different sections, each with its own prayers to complement brief daily readings from Sacred Scripture, *The Imitation of Christ* by Thomas à Kempis, and Montfort's own work, *True Devotion to the Blessed Virgin*. This is how the days will be divided:

- **12 Day Preparation – Days 1-12**
  First comes a 12 day preparation period that consists of emptying oneself of the spirit of the world in penance and mortification. For these 12 days, we pray the Veni Creator, the Ave Maris Stella, the Magnificat, and the Glory Be.

- **Week One – Days 13-19**
  The first week focuses on offering up our prayers and devotions for the purpose of coming to understand ourselves and our sins. Humility is the key. For this week, we pray the Litany of the Holy Ghost, the Litany of Loreto, and the Ave Maris Stella.

- **Week Two – Days 20-26**
  During the second week, we ask the Holy Ghost to help us better understand the Blessed Virgin. We pray the Litany of the Holy Ghost, the Litany of Loreto, the Ave Maris Stellis, the prayer to Mary by St. Louis de Montfort. We also add 5 decades of the Holy Rosary each day for assistance.

- **Week Three – Days 27-33**
  During the third week, we seek to better understand Christ through meditation and the Litany of the Holy Ghost, the Ave Maris Stella, and the Litany of the

Holy Name of Jesus, Montfort's prayer to Jesus, and the prayer, O Jesus Living in Mary.

- **Consecration Day – Day 34**

Don't just read the readings, internalize them. Don't let your lips just mouth the prayers; truly pray them. Just saying the words won't work; it's not a magic incantation.

You may feel less motivated or less focused some days, but persevere. You may even miss a day. Keep going. Keep trying.

12 Day Preparation

Prayers said daily during the consecration are provided in an appendix at the end of the text.

Day 1

Examine your conscience, pray, and practice renouncement of your own will. This mortification results in purity of heart.

This purity is the indispensable condition for contemplating God in heaven, to see Him on earth and to know Him by the light of faith. The first part of the preparation should be employed in casting off the spirit of the world which is contrary to that of Jesus Christ. The spirit of the world consists essentially in the denial of the supreme dominion of God. This denial is manifested in practice by sin and disobedience. Thus, it is principally opposed to the spirit of Christ, which is also that of Mary.

It manifests itself by the concupiscence of the flesh, by the concupiscence of the eyes, and by the pride of life, and by disobedience to God's laws and the abuse of created things. Its works are the following: sin in all forms, then all else by which the devil leads to sin; works which bring error and darkness to the mind, and seduction and corruption to the will. Its pomps are the splendor and the charms employed by the devil to render sin alluring in persons, places, and things.

Reading: The Gospel of Matthew 5:1-19

And seeing the multitudes, he went up into a mountain, and when he was set down, his disciples came unto him. And opening his mouth, he taught them, saying:

Blessed are the poor in spirit: for theirs is the kingdom of heaven.
Blessed are the meek: for they shall possess the land.
Blessed are they that mourn: for they shall be comforted.
Blessed are they that hunger and thirst after justice: for they shall have their fill.
Blessed are the merciful: for they shall obtain mercy.
Blessed are the clean of heart: for they shall see God.
Blessed are the peacemakers: for they shall be called children of God.
Blessed are they that suffer persecution for justice' sake: for theirs is the kingdom of heaven.
Blessed are ye when they shall revile you, and persecute you, and speak all that is evil against you, untruly, for my sake: Be glad and rejoice, for your reward is very great in heaven. For so they persecuted the prophets that were before you.

You are the salt of the earth. But if the salt lose its savour, wherewith shall it be salted? It is good for nothing any more but to be cast out, and to be trodden on by men. You are the light of the world. A city seated on a mountain cannot be hid. Neither do men light a candle and put it under a bushel, but upon a candlestick, that it may shine to all that are in the house. So let your light shine before men, that they may see your good works, and glorify your Father who is in heaven.

Do not think that I am come to destroy the law, or the prophets. I am not come to destroy, but to fulfill. For amen I say unto you, till heaven and earth pass, one jot, or one tittle shall not pass of the law, till all be fulfilled. He therefore that shall break one of these least commandments, and shall so teach men, shall be called the least in the kingdom of heaven. But he that shall do and teach, he shall be called great in the kingdom of heaven.

Daily Prayers to Recite: Veni Creator, Ave Maris Stella, Magnificat, and Glory Be (see text of prayers at end of text)

DAY 2

Reading: The Gospel of Matthew 5:48, 6:1-15

Jesus said: "You, therefore, must be perfect, as your heavenly Father is perfect."

"Beware of practicing your piety before men in order to be seen by them; for then you will have no reward from your Father who is in heaven."

"Thus, when you give alms, sound no trumpet before you, as the hypocrites do in the synagogues and in the streets, that they may be praised by men. Truly, I say to you, they have their reward. But when you give alms, do not let your left hand know what your right hand is doing, so that your alms may be in secret; and your Father who sees in secret will reward you."

"And when you pray, you must not be like the hypocrites; for they love to stand and pray in the synagogues and at the street corners, that they may be seen by men. Truly, I say to you, they have their reward. But when you pray, go into your room and shut the door and pray to your Father who is in secret; and your Father who sees in secret will reward you."

"And in praying do not heap up empty phrases as the Gentiles do; for they think that they will be heard for their many words. Do not be like them, for your Father knows what you need before you ask him. Pray then like this:

Our Father who art in heaven,
Hallowed be thy name.
Thy kingdom come,
Thy will be done,
   On earth as it is in heaven.
Give us this day our daily bread;
And forgive us our debts,
   As we also have forgiven our debtors;
And lead us not into temptation,
   But deliver us from evil."

"For if you forgive men their trespasses, your heavenly Father also will forgive you; but if you do not forgive men their trespasses, neither will your Father forgive your trespasses."

"And when you fast, do not look dismal, like the hypocrites, for they disfigure their faces that their fasting may be seen by men. Truly, I say to you, they have their reward. But when you fast, anoint your head and wash your face, that your fasting may not be seen by men but by your Father who is in secret; and your Father who sees in secret will reward you."

Daily Prayers to Recite: Veni Creator, Ave Maris Stella, Magnificat, and Glory Be (see text of prayers at end of text)

DAY 3

Reading: The Gospel of Matthew 7:1-14

Jesus said: "Judge not, that you be not judged. For with the judgment you pronounce you will be judged, and the measure you give will be the measure you get. Why do you see the speck that is in your brother's eye, but do not notice the log that is in your own eye? Or how can you say to your brother, 'Let me take the speck out of your eye,' when there is the log in your own eye? You hypocrite, first take the log out of your own eye, and then you will see clearly to take the speck out of your brother's eye."

"Do not give dogs what is holy; and do not throw your pearls before swine, lest they trample them under foot and turn to attack you."

"Ask, and it will be given you; seek, and you will find; knock, and it will be opened to you. For every one who asks receives, and he who seeks finds, and to him who knocks it will be opened. Or what man of you, if his son asks him for bread, will give him a stone? Or if he asks for a fish, will give him a serpent? If you then, who are evil, know how to give good gifts to your children, how much more will your Father who is in heaven give good things to those who ask him! So whatever you wish that men would do to you, do so to them; for this is the law and the prophets."

"Enter by the narrow gate; for the gate is wide and the way is easy, that leads to destruction, and those who enter by it are many. For the gate is narrow and the way is hard, that leads to life, and those who find it are few."

Daily Prayers to Recite: Veni Creator, Ave Maris Stella, Magnificat, and Glory Be (see text of prayers at end of text)

DAY 4

Reading: *Imitation of Christ* by Thomas á Kempis, Book III, Chapters 7, 40

That man has no good of himself, that he cannot glory in anything, Lord, what is man, that You are mindful of him? Or the son of man, that You visit him? What has man deserved that You should give him grace? Lord, what cause have I to complain, if You forsake me? Or what can I justly accuse, if You do not grant my petitions?

I may truly think and say this most assuredly: Lord I am nothing. I can do nothing by myself that is good. I am in all things defective and ever tend to nothing. Unless I am assisted and interiorly instructed by You, I become wholly tepid and relaxed. But You, O Lord, are unchanging and endure unto eternity. You are ever good, just and holy, doing all things well, justly, holily, and wisely.

But I am changing, having failed so many times, and am more inclined to go back, than to go forward. But, if You please, when You stretch out Your helping hand, it quickly becomes better. For You alone, far beyond the help of any man, can assist me and so strengthen me. Nothing so changes my demeanor and converts my heart, as the rest I find in You alone.

He who is too secure in time of peace is often too dejected in time of war. If you could just remember yourself as humble and little, and if you could keep your spirit ordered, you would not fall so easily into danger and offense. It is wise to remember: when you make your plans in the fervor of summertime, how it will be when the light is withdrawn.

Daily Prayers to Recite: Veni Creator, Ave Maris Stella, Magnificat, and Glory Be (see text of prayers at end of text)

DAY 5

Reading: *Imitation of Christ* by Thomas á Kempis, Book III, Chapters 7, 40

If only I could cast from myself all human comfort. I would flee comfort either for the sake of devotion, or because nothing else can comfort me and I am compelled to seek You. Then, I might deservedly hope for Your favor and rejoice in the gift of a new consolation.

As often as it happens, I will give thanks to God from Whom all things proceed. Because, try as I might, I am but vanity and nothing in Your sight. I am an inconstant and weak man. I cannot glory in myself and on what basis, should I desire to be thought of highly? Only perhaps my very nothingness, and even this is most vain.

Such vanity is an evil plague, because it distracts us from true glory and robs us of heavenly grace. For, while a man takes complacency in himself, he displeases You. While he wants for human applause, he is deprived of true virtues.

True glory and holy exultation is to glory in You, and not in one's self. True glory is to rejoice in Your Name, but not in one's own strength. To find pleasure in no creature, except for Your sake.

Let Your Name be praised, not mine. Let Your work be magnified, not mine. Let Your Holy Name be blessed, but let me not seek the praise of men. You are my glory. You are the praise of my heart. In You, I will glory and rejoice forever; but for myself, I will glory in nothing but in my infirmities.

Daily Prayers to Recite: Veni Creator, Ave Maris Stella, Magnificat, and Glory Be (see text of prayers at end of text)

DAY 6

Reading: *Imitation of Christ* by Thomas á Kempis, Book I, Chapters 18

Look upon the bold examples of the Saints. Real perfection in the religious life shines in their lives. And you will see how little, almost nothing, that we do nowadays compares with them.

What are our lives compared with theirs? Saints and friends of Christ, they served our Lord in hunger and in thirst, in cold, in nakedness, in labor and in weariness, in watching and waiting, in fasting, prayers and holy meditations, and in frequent persecutions and reproaches.

How many terrible tribulations did the Apostles suffer? And the Martyrs, Confessors, Virgins, and all the rest who resolved to follow in the steps of Christ! They willingly offered their lives in this world, that they might have life everlasting.

What a strict and self-renouncing life, the Desert Fathers led! What long and grievous temptations they bore! To think how often were they harassed by the Devil, how frequent and fervent were the prayers they offered to God, and what rigorous abstinence they practiced.

Think how valiantly they battled to subdue their imperfections. Think how pure was their dedication to God. They labored by day and spent most of the night in prayer. Even while they labored, their minds were at prayer. They spent all their time profitably. Every hour seemed short when spent with God.

They forgot even basic bodily needs in the great sweetness of contemplation. They renounced all riches, dignities, honors, and kindred, taking hardly even what was necessary for life. It grieved them to serve the body even in its necessity. Accordingly, they were poor in earthly things, but very rich in grace and virtues.

Daily Prayers to Recite: Veni Creator, Ave Maris Stella, Magnificat, and Glory Be (see text of prayers at end of text)

DAY 7

Reading: *Imitation of Christ* by Thomas á Kempis, Book I, Chapters 18 continued

Outwardly, the Desert Fathers suffered want. Inwardly, they were refreshed with grace and Divine consolation. To the world, they were aliens and strange and despised. To God, they were dear and beloved friends.

In them shined all the perfection of virtue: they persevered in true humility. They lived in simple obedience. They walked in charity and patience. And so, every day they advanced in spirit and gained great grace with God. They are an example to all religious people. Their lives should stir us all to devotion. Their example should excite us to grow in grace and virtue. It should not be the example of the lukewarm, the dissolute, and the idle that we follow into vice and distraction.

How great was the fervor of the early religious fathers while still in the dawn of Christianity and the beginning of monasticism! How great was their devotion in prayer, and their zeal for virtue. How great was the discipline, reverence, and obedience that flourished under the rule of their superiors. Their deeds still bear witness to this day that they, who battled for holiness and perfection, trampled the world beneath their feet.

Nowadays, all it takes for a man to be considered great and virtuous is to avoid public shame. To be exceptional, a man needs only to keep a little spark of his original fervor alive. A memory of a conversion is enough, when it is ongoing conversion which is so desperately needed. How lukewarm and pitiful is our current state! How quickly we fall away after that retreat or mountaintop experience. We grow tried with our lives because of sloth and meekness. Out of negligence, we let the fire of God's magnificence grow stale. Just think of how we must afflict Jesus, who has seen so often, and even in us, the fire of the great saints.

Daily Prayers to Recite: Veni Creator, Ave Maris Stella, Magnificat, and Glory Be (see text of prayers at end of text)

DAY 8

Reading: *Imitation of Christ* by Thomas á Kempis, Book I, Chapters 13

For as long as we live in this world, temptations and tribulations will be our constant companions. As it is written in Job, "Man's life on earth is a temptation." Otherwise translated, "Man's life on earth is warfare." This war requires that every man be on guard about his temptations and watchful in prayer. Or else, the devil, who never sleeps but is always prowling about and seeking to devour, will deceive him and catch him.

No man is so perfect and holy as to be wholly free of temptation. Nevertheless, temptations are very profitable to man *when we wrestle with them.* Though troublesome and painful they may be, temptations humble, purify, and instruct us. All the Saints who now wear crowns in Heaven wrestled through many tribulations and temptations and were purified by them. Those who surrendered, who could not bear to wrestle with their temptations, fell away and are now Hell's prisoners.

Many seek to flee temptations, and fall worse into them. Instead of cleaving to Christ, they fall into the devil's embrace. This battle cannot be won by fleeing the battlefield. Only with patience and true humility, we overcome our enemies.

A man gains little profit by merely fleeing the outward occasions of sin. He must pluck pluck out the root, the disordered desires hidden away in our hearts. Like weeds, temptations will come back again and again, growing in strength each time. Little by little, however, with patience, fortitude, and God's grace, you will sooner overcome temptations than by relying on your own strength and gritted teeth.

In your temptation, take counsel with an accountability partner or spiritual director. These should not deal harshly with one who is tempted. Instead, they should pour out consolation and comfort, just as they would want to be comforted.

The beginning of all temptations is inconstancy of mind and too little confidence in God. Just as a ship, without rudder or helm, will be driven off course by every storm, so the man who neglects his resolutions will soon lose sight of his guiding star when buffeted by waves of temptation.

Daily Prayers to Recite: Veni Creator, Ave Maris Stella, Magnificat, and Glory Be (see text of prayers at end of text)

DAY 9

Reading: *Imitation of Christ* by Thomas á Kempis, Book I, Chapter 13 continued

Fire purifies gold, and temptation purifies the righteous man. We often do not know what we are capable of. Temptation, however, shows us plainly.

We must be watchful, especially at the beginning of a temptation. It is then that the enemy is most easily overcome. We cannot let the devil enter the door of the mind. We must hold him back at the threshold the very moment he knocks. As the saying goes, "Resist beginnings; all too late the cure."

First comes an unclean thought into the mind. Then comes a strong phantasm of imagination. Delight and pleasure follow, and then various evil motions. By the end, there is full consent. So, little by little, the devil gains entrance, if he is not resisted in the beginning. The slower a man is to resist, the weaker his resistance becomes, and the devil is daily stronger against him.

Some suffer grievous temptations in the beginning of their conversion, and some suffer at the end. Some are troubled nearly their whole life, and some are only ever tempted very lightly. This is all according to the wisdom and equity of God. God weighs each man's condition and merits and ordains all things for the salvation of His elect.

Therefore, we must not despair when we are tempted. Instead, pray all the more fervently to God that in his infinite goodness and fatherly pity, he will help us overcome every temptation. God will, as St. Paul said, go before us in grace, so we are able to withstand the temptation.

Let us, then, humble ourselves under the strong hand of Almighty God in every temptation. God will save and exalt those who are meek and humble in spirit. For again, a man is proven in temptation, as is the progress he has made. His merit shines before God and his virtue is made manifest.

Daily Prayers to Recite: Veni Creator, Ave Maris Stella, Magnificat, and Glory Be (see text of prayers at end of text)

DAY 10

Reading: *Imitation of Christ* by Thomas á Kempis, Book III, Chapter 10, "That it is sweet to forsake the world and to serve God"

I will speak again to you, my Lord Jesus, and I will not be silent. I will speak into the ears of my Lord, my God and my King, Who is on high:

How great is Your sweetness, O Lord, which You have hidden for those that fear You! But what are You to those who love You? What are You to those who serve You with their whole heart? Truly, it is the unspeakable sweetness of contemplation, which You have bestowed on those who love You.

In this most of all, You have showed me the sweetness of Your love, that when I had no being, You made me. And when I was straying far from You, You brought me back again, that I might serve You. And You have commanded me to serve You.

Fountain of everlasting love, what shall I say of You? How can I forget You, Who remembered me even after I was dead and lost? Beyond all hope, You showed mercy to Your servant. Without deserving it, You gave me Your mercy and friendship. But what can I give you in return for such gifts?

Not all men are granted leave to forsake all things, to renounce the world, and to live a solitary, monastic life. Is it much that I should serve You, when all of creation is bound to do the same? It doesn't seem like much to serve You. What does seem extraordinary is that You would receive such a wretched and unworthy man as me into your service.

It is a great honor and a great glory to serve You and despise all things for You. Those who willingly subject themselves to Your holy service will receive great grace. Those who cast aside all carnal pleasures out of love for You will experience the Holy Spirit and the sweetest of consolations.

Daily Prayers to Recite: Veni Creator, Ave Maris Stella, Magnificat, and Glory Be (see text of prayers at end of text)

DAY 11

Reading: *Imitation of Christ* by Thomas á Kempis, Book I, Chapter 25, "On the Fervent Amendment of our Whole Life"

There was once an anxious man, who often wavered between hope and fear and doubted whether he was in a state of grace. The man threw himself to the ground in prayer before one of the altars in the church and said "Oh, if I only knew if I will persevere in virtue until my death."

That very instant the man heard within him a heavenly answer: "And if you did know this, what would you do? Do now what you would do then, and you will be saved."

The man was immediately comforted and he committed himself wholly to the Divine Will. From then on, his anxious thoughts ceased. His curiosity no longer dwelled over what would happen to him. Instead, he spent his energy discerning God's will for his life. He sought to begin and end each of his deeds to the pleasure of God.

"Trust in the Lord and do good deeds," says the Prophet David. "Inhabit the land, and you shall feed from its riches."

There is one thing in particular that stops many men from progressing in the spiritual life and amending their lives. It is the false worldly fear of the pain and labor which is needed in the struggle to win virtue. Those who strive the most manfully to overcome their most difficult vices will most quickly advance in virtue. A man profits most and wins the most grace when he tackles those things in which he most has to overcome himself.

All men do not, indeed, have equal difficulties to overcome. Some men have greater passions than others. Nevertheless, a zealous lover of God, even if he has stronger passions, will also make a stronger advance in virtue. The man of great passion will make greater progress than he of little passion, who is less fervent toward virtue.

Two things greatly help a man amend his life: (1) a strong withdrawal from himself and from those things which his body most craves, and (2) a fervent labor for the virtues he most needs.

Daily Prayers to Recite: Veni Creator, Ave Maris Stella, Magnificat, and Glory Be (see text of prayers at end of text)

DAY 12

Reading: *Imitation of Christ* by Thomas á Kempis, Book I, Chapter 25, continued

Work especially to overcome those vices in yourself, which most disturb you in others. Wherever you go, profit from the example of others. When you observe virtuous examples, emulate them. When you observe vicious examples, avoid them. As you consider the work of others, remember also that your works, too, are being observed.

How sweet and pleasing it is, to see our brothers who fervent and devout, obedient and well-taught. How sad and grievous it is, to see our brothers who walk disordered paths, not applying themselves to that for which they are made. How hurtful it is, to see our brothers neglect their calling and neglect those who have been entrusted to their care, and set their minds to what is forbidden.

Be mindful of the purpose that has been set before you. Set always before you the image of Christ Crucified. If you lovingly behold Jesus' afflicted face, you may well be ashamed. Ashamed that you have not better conformed your life to His, despite all the time you have been on the way of God.

A man should inwardly and seriously exercise himself in the most holy life and passion of our Lord. He will find there abundantly all he needs. Neither will he need to seek anywhere else, apart from Jesus. If only Jesus crucified were more often in our hearts and minds, how quickly we would be filled with everything we need. A fervent and diligent man is thus prepared for all things and cheerfully obedient to all God's commands.

Resisting vices and temptations is harder work than the toil and sweat of physical labor. A man who does not fight the little sins, little by little, will fall into the greater sins. You will always rejoice in the evening, if you have spent your day profitably avoiding and conquering sin.

Be watchful of yourself. Stir yourself up for devotion. Admonish yourself against sin and ruin. And whatever you do for others, do not forget to do for yourself. The more violently you fight against your own will and for God's will, the more you will advance in virtue.

Daily Prayers to Recite: Veni Creator, Ave Maris Stella, Magnificat, and Glory Be (see text of prayers at end of text)

FIRST WEEK

DAY 13

Theme for the Week: Knowledge of Self

All that you do this week: prayers, examinations, reflection, acts of renouncing our own will, acts of contrition for our sins, acts of contempt of self. All these should be performed at the feet of Mary.

Imagine yourself putting all these things at Mary's precious feet. We pray that we will come to know ourselves in her light, who is the immaculate reflection of Jesus. Near her, we will be able to behold the abyss of our miseries without despairing.

All our pious actions should be directed to a special request: *for a knowledge of ourselves and for contrition for our sins, and that we should do and receive all this in a spirit of piety.* During this period, we will focus not so much on the opposition between the spirit of Jesus and our own. Rather, we pray to grasp fully the miserable and humiliating state to which our sins have reduced us.

The True Devotion to Mary is an easy, short, sure, and perfect way to arrive at complete and perfect union with Our Lord Jesus. Nevertheless, to enter seriously upon this path, we need to be strongly convinced of the misery caused by our sins and our own helplessness. This is why we must attain this knowledge of ourselves.

Reading: The Gospel of Luke, 11:1-10

He was praying in a certain place, and when he ceased, one of his disciples said to him, "Lord, teach us to pray, as John taught his disciples." And he said to them, "When you pray, say:

> Father, hallowed be thy name. Thy kingdom come. Give us each day our daily bread; and forgive us our sins, for we ourselves forgive everyone who is indebted to us; and lead us not into temptation.

And he said to them, "Which of you who has a friend will go to him at midnight and say to him, 'Friend, lend me three loaves; for a friend of mine has arrived on a journey, and I have nothing to set before him'; and he will answer from within, 'Do not bother me; the door is now shut, and my children are with me in bed; I cannot get up and give you anything'? I tell you, though he will not get up and give him anything because he is his friend, yet because of his importunity he will rise and give him whatever he needs."

"And I tell you, Ask, and it will be given you; seek, and you will find; knock, and it will be opened to you. For every one who asks receives, and he who seeks finds, and to him who knocks it will be opened."

"What father among you, if his son asks for a fish, will instead of a fish give him a serpent; or if he asks for an egg, will give him a scorpion? If you then, who are evil, know how to give good gifts to your children, how much more will the heavenly Father give the Holy Spirit to those who ask him!"

Daily Prayers to Recite: Litany of the Holy Ghost, Litany of the Blessed Virgin Mary, and Ave Maris Stella (see text of prayers at end of text)

DAY 14

Reading: *Imitation of Christ* by Thomas á Kempis, Book III, Chapter 13, "Of the Obedience of One in Humble Subjection, After the Example of Jesus Christ"

My son, says the Lord Jesus Christ, he who endeavors to withdraw himself from obedience, withdraws himself from grace, cf. Matt. 16:24. He who seeks possessions for himself, loses those which is given to all.

If a man doesn't cheerfully and freely submit himself to his superior, it is a sign that his flesh is not yet perfectly obedient to him. Such a man's flesh kicks and murmurs against him. Therefore, if you truly desire to overcome yourself and make your flesh obedient to your spirit, learn first to obey you superiors.

The outward enemy is sooner overcome if the inner man – the soul – is not feeble and weak. There is no greater or more troublesome enemy to the soul than *you*, if your flesh is not in harmony with your spirit. You must, therefore, develop a contempt for yourself, if you desire to prevail against your flesh and blood. To the same degree you love yourself inordinately, you will fear to resign yourself to another's will.

Is it so great a matter for a man, who is but dust from nothing, to subject himself to another for God's sake, when I, the Almighty and the Most High God, who created all things from nothing, humbly subjected Myself to man for your sake? I made myself the humblest and lowest of all men (Luke 2:7; John 13:14), that you might overcome your pride with My humility.

O dust! Learn to be obedient. Learn to humble yourself, who are but earth and clay. Learn to bow down under the feet of all men for My sake. Learn to break your will and to be subject to all from the heart.

Daily Prayers to Recite: Litany of the Holy Ghost, Litany of the Blessed Virgin Mary, and Ave Maris Stella (see text of prayers at end of text)

DAY 15

Reading 1: Luke 13:1-5, "Repent or Perish"

There were some present at that very time who told him of the Galileans whose blood Pilate had mingled with their sacrifices. And he answered them, "Do you think that these Galileans were worse sinners than all the other Galileans, because they suffered thus? I tell you, No; but unless you repent you will all likewise perish. Or those eighteen upon whom the tower in Silo'am fell and killed them, do you think that they were worse offenders than all the others who dwelt in Jerusalem? I tell you, No; but unless you repent you will all likewise perish."

Reading 2: *True Devotion to the Blessed Virgin Mary*, Nos. 81 and 82, "We Need Mary in order to Die to Ourselves"

Secondly, in order to empty ourselves of self, we must die daily to ourselves. This involves our renouncing what the powers of the soul and the senses of the body incline us to do. We must see as if we did not see, hear as if we did not hear, and use the things of this world as if we did not use them.

This is what St. Paul calls "dying daily". Unless the grain of wheat falls to the ground and dies, it remains only a single grain and does not bear any good fruit. We must die to self and our holiest devotions must lead us to this necessary and fruitful death. Otherwise, we shall not bear fruit of any worth and our devotions will cease to be profitable. All our good works will be tainted by self-love and self-will. Our greatest sacrifices and our best actions, then, will be unacceptable to God.

Consequently, when we die, we shall find ourselves devoid of virtue and merit. We will discover that we do not possess even one spark of that pure love which God shares only with those who have died to themselves and whose life is hidden within Jesus Christ.

Thirdly, we must choose among all the devotions to the Blessed Virgin the one which will lead us more surely to this dying to self. This devotion will be the best and the most sanctifying for us.

Daily Prayers to Recite: Litany of the Holy Ghost, Litany of the Blessed Virgin Mary, and Ave Maris Stella (see text of prayers at end of text)

DAY 16

Reading 1: *True Devotion To the Blessed Virgin Mary*, No. 228, "Preparatory Exercises"

During the first week, we offered up all our prayers and acts of devotion to acquire knowledge of ourselves and sorrow for our sins. We are to perform all our actions in a spirit of humility. With this end in view, we may, if we wish, meditate on what St. Louis de Montfort has said concerning our corrupted nature, and consider ourselves during six days of the week as nothing but sails, slugs, toads, swine, snakes, and goats.

Or else, we may meditate on the following three considerations of St. Bernard: "Remember what you were: corrupted seed.
Remember what you are: a body destined for decay.
Remember what you will be: food for worms."

Ask our Lord and the Holy Spirit to enlighten you saying, "Lord, that I may see," or "Lord, let me know myself," or "Come, Holy Spirit." Every day we should say the "Litany of the Holy Spirit." We will then turn to our Blessed Lady and beg her to obtain for us that great grace which is the foundation of all others, the grace of self-knowledge. For this intention, we will say each day the "Ave Maris Stella" and the "Litany of the Blessed Virgin."

Reading 2: *Imitation of Christ* by Thomas á Kempis, Book II, Chapter 5, "Of Self-consideration"

We cannot trust in ourselves or in our intelligence too much, because we often lacking in grace and understanding, c.f. Jer. 17:5. Precious little light is there in us, and too often we lose this through neglect. We do not see or even want to see just how blind we are. Oftentimes we do evil and then try to defend ourselves, doing even greater harm, c.f. Psalm 141:4.

Sometimes, too, we are moved with passion and mistake it as zeal from God. We passionately admonish small faults in our neighbors and ignore far greater faults in ourselves, c.f. Matt. 7:5. We may ruminate over the wrongs we suffer at the hands of others and ignore the suffering we have inflicted on others. He that well and rightly considers his own works, will find little cause to judge harshly of another.

Daily Prayers to Recite: Litany of the Holy Ghost, Litany of the Blessed Virgin Mary, and Ave Maris Stella (see text of prayers at end of text)

DAY 17

Reading 1: *True Devotion To the Blessed Virgin Mary*, No. 228, "Preparatory Exercises" continued

Regarding judgment and the punishment of sinners, in all things look to the end. How will you stand before that strict Judge (Heb. 10:31) before whom nothing is hid? This Judge is not appeased with gifts and allows no excuses, but will judge according to right.

O wretched and foolish sinner! You, who can be terrified by the look of an angry man, what answer will you make to God who knows all your wickedness (Job 9:2)? Why do you not provide for yourself (Luke 16:9) for the day of judgment? On that day, no man can be excused or defended by another. On that day, every one must carry their own burdens.

Reading 2: Luke 16:1-8, "The Crafty Steward" or "The Parable of the Dishonest Manager"

Jesus also said to the disciples, "There was a rich man who had a steward, and charges were brought to him that this man was wasting his goods. And he called him and said to him, 'What is this that I hear about you? Turn in the account of your stewardship, for you can no longer be steward.' And the steward said to himself, 'What shall I do, since my master is taking the stewardship away from me? I am not strong enough to dig, and I am ashamed to beg. I have decided what to do, so that people may receive me into their houses when I am put out of the stewardship.'

So, summoning his master's debtors one by one, he said to the first, 'How much do you owe my master?' He said, 'A hundred measures of oil.' And he said to him, 'Take your bill, and sit down quickly and write fifty.' Then he said to another, 'And how much do you owe?' He said, 'A hundred measures of wheat.' He said to him, 'Take your bill, and write eighty.' The master commended the dishonest steward for his prudence; for the sons of this world are wiser in their own generation than the sons of light.

Daily Prayers to Recite: Litany of the Holy Ghost, Litany of the Blessed Virgin Mary, and Ave Maris Stella (see text of prayers at end of text)

DAY 18

Reading 1: Gospel of Luke 17:1-10

On Leading Others Astray
And he said to his disciples, "Temptations to sin are sure to come; but woe to him by whom they come! It would be better for him if a millstone were hung round his neck and he

147

were cast into the sea, than that he should cause one of these little ones to sin."

On Brotherly Correction
"Take heed to yourselves; if your brother sins, rebuke him, and if he repents, forgive him; and if he sins against you seven times in the day, and turns to you seven times, and says, 'I repent,' you must forgive him."

The Power of Faith
The Apostles said to the Lord, "Increase our faith!" And the Lord said, "If you had faith as a grain of mustard seed, you could say to this mulberry tree, 'Be rooted up, and be planted in the sea,' and it would obey you."

Humble Service
"Will any one of you, who has a servant plowing or keeping sheep, say to him when he has come in from the field, 'Come at once and sit down at table'? Will he not rather say to him, 'Prepare supper for me, and gird yourself and serve me, till I eat and drink; and afterward you shall eat and drink'? Does he thank the servant because he did what was commanded? So you also, when you have done all that is commanded you, say, 'We are unworthy servants; we have only done what was our duty.'"

Reading 2: *Imitation of Christ* by Thomas á Kempis, Book III, Chapter 47, "That All Grievous Things are to be Suffered Joyfully for the Sake of Eternal Life"

My son, says the Lord, do not be wearied by the labors you have undertaken for My sake. Do not let tribulation cast you into despair. Instead, let My promise strengthen and comfort you in every circumstance. I am well able to reward you beyond all measure and imagination. You will not toil for long here, nor will you always be oppressed with grief. Await my promises, and you will see an end to all your trials.

Daily Prayers to Recite: Litany of the Holy Ghost, Litany of the Blessed Virgin Mary, and Ave Maris Stella (see text of prayers at end of text)

DAY 19

Reading: Gospel of Luke 18:15-30

Jesus Blesses Little Children
Now they were bringing even infants to him that he might touch them; and when the disciples saw it, they rebuked them. But Jesus called them to him, saying, "Let the children come to me, and do not hinder them; for to such belongs the kingdom of God. Truly, I say to you, whoever does not receive the kingdom of God like a child shall not enter it."

The Rich Young Ruler
And a ruler asked him, "Good Teacher, what shall I do to inherit eternal life?" And Jesus said to him, "Why do you call me good? No one is good but God alone. You know the commandments: 'Do not commit adultery, Do not kill, Do not steal, Do not bear false witness, Honor your father and mother.'" And he said, "All these I have observed from my youth." And when Jesus heard it, he said to him, "One thing you still lack. Sell all that you have and distribute to the poor, and you will have treasure in heaven; and come, follow me." But when he heard this he became sad, for he was very rich.

The Danger of Riches

149

Jesus looking at him became sorrowful and said, "How hard it is for those who have riches to enter the kingdom of God! For it is easier for a camel to go through the eye of a needle than for a rich man to enter the kingdom of God." Those who heard it said, "Then who can be saved?" But he said, "What is impossible with men is possible with God."

The Reward of Renunciation
And Peter said, "Lo, we have left our homes and followed you." And he said to them, "Truly, I say to you, there is no man who has left house or wife or brothers or parents or children, for the sake of the kingdom of God, who will not receive manifold more in this time, and in the age to come eternal life."

Daily Prayers to Recite: Daily Prayers to Recite: Litany of the Holy Ghost, Litany of the Blessed Virgin Mary, and Ave Maris Stella (see text of prayers at end of text)

SECOND WEEK

DAY 20

Theme for the Week: Knowledge of The Blessed Virgin

Acts of love, pious affection for the Blessed Virgin, imitation of her virtues, especially her profound humility, her lively faith, her blind obedience, her continual mental prayer, her mortification in all things, her surpassing purity, her ardent charity, her heroic patience, her angelic sweetness, and her divine wisdom: "there being," as St. Louis de Montfort says, "the ten principal virtues of the Blessed Virgin."

We must unite ourselves to Jesus through Mary. This is the principal characteristic of our devotion. Saint Louis de Montfort, therefore, asks that we employ ourselves in acquiring a knowledge of the Blessed Virgin.

Mary is our sovereign and our mediatrix, our Mother and our Mistress. Let us then endeavor to know the effects of this royalty, of this mediation, and of this maternity, as well as the grandeurs and prerogatives which are the foundation or consequences thereof. Our Mother is also a perfect mold wherein we are to be molded in order to make her intentions and dispositions ours. This we cannot achieve without studying the interior life of Mary. This means her virtues, her sentiments, her actions, her participation in the mysteries of Christ, and her union with Him.

Reading: Luke 2:16-21, 45-52

And they went with haste, and found Mary and Joseph, and the babe lying in a manger. And when they saw it they made known the saying which had been told them concerning this child; and all who heard it wondered at what the shepherds told them. But Mary kept all these things, pondering them in her heart. And the shepherds returned, glorifying and praising God for all they had heard and seen, as it had been told them.

And at the end of eight days, when he was circumcised, he was called Jesus, the name given by the angel before he was conceived in the womb.

[...] and when they did not find him, they returned to Jerusalem, seeking him. After three days they found him in the temple, sitting among the teachers, listening to them and asking them questions; and all who heard him were amazed at his understanding and his answers. And when they saw him they were astonished; and his mother said to him, "Son, why have you treated us so? Behold, your father and I have been looking for you anxiously." And he said to them, "How is it that you sought me? Did you not know that I must be in my Father's house?" And they did not understand the saying which he spoke to them. And he went down with them and came to Nazareth, and was obedient to them; and his mother kept all these things in her heart.

And Jesus increased in wisdom and in stature, and in favor with God and man.

Daily Prayers to Recite: Litany of the Holy Ghost, Litany of the Blessed Virgin Mary, Ave Maris Stella, St. Louis de Montfort's Prayer to Mary, and the Rosary (see text of prayers at end of text; see Chapter 2 for instructions on reciting the Rosary)

DAY 21

Reading: *True Devotion to the Blessed Virgin Mary*, Nos. 23-24

If we would go up to God and be united with Him, we must use *the same means* that He used to come down to us, to be made Man, and to impart His graces to us. This means is a true devotion to our Blessed Lady.

There are several true devotions to our Lady. I do not speak here of those which are false. The **first** consists in fulfilling our Christian duties, avoiding mortal sin, acting more out of love than fear, praying to our Lady now and then, and honoring her as the Mother of God – but without having any special devotion to her.

The **second** consists in fostering more perfect love for our Lady, as well as confidence and veneration. Such leads us to join the Confraternities of the Holy Rosary and of the Scapular, to recite the five or fifteen decades of the Holy Rosary, to honor Mary's images and altars, to publish her praises and to enroll ourselves in her modalities. This devotion is good, holy, and praiseworthy if we keep ourselves free from sin. But even this is not so perfect as the next. Nor is this way as efficient in severing our soul from creatures. That is, in detaching ourselves in order to be united with Jesus Christ.

The **third** devotion to our Lady, known and practiced by very few persons, is what I am about to disclose to you, whose soul is fixed on Heaven. It consists in giving one's self entirely and as a slave to Mary, and to Jesus through Mary, and after that, to do all that we do, through Mary, with Mary, in Mary, and for Mary.

We should choose a special feast day on which we give, consecrate, and sacrifice to Mary voluntarily, lovingly, and without constraint, entirely and without reserve the following:

- Our body and soul;
- Our families;
- Our exterior property, such as house and income; and
- Our interior and spiritual possessions, such as our merits, graces, virtues, and satisfactions.

Daily Prayers to Recite: Litany of the Holy Ghost, Litany of the Blessed Virgin Mary, Ave Maris Stella, St. Louis de Montfort's Prayer to Mary, and the Rosary (see text of prayers at end of text; see Chapter 2 for instructions on reciting the Rosary)

DAY 22

Reading: *True Devotion to the Blessed Virgin Mary*, Nos. 106-110, "Marks of authentic devotion to our Lady"

106. First, true devotion to our Lady is **interior**. It comes from within the mind and the heart and follows from the esteem in which we hold her, the high regard we have for her greatness, and the love we bear her.

107. Second, it is **trustful**. It fills us with confidence in the Blessed Virgin, the confidence that a child has for its loving Mother. It prompts us to go to her in every need of body and soul with great simplicity, trust, and affection.

108. Third, true devotion to our Lady is **holy**. It leads us to avoid sin and to imitate the virtues of Mary. Her ten principal virtues are deep humility, lively faith, blind obedience, unceasing prayer, constant self-denial, surpassing purity, ardent love, heroic patience, angelic kindness, and heavenly wisdom.

109. Fourth, true devotion to our Lady is **constant**. It strengthens us in our desire to do good and prevents us from giving up our devotional practices too easily. It gives us the courage to oppose the fashions and maxims of the world, the vexations and unruly inclinations of the flesh, and the temptations of the devil. Thus, a person truly devoted to our Blessed Lady is not changeable, fretful, scrupulous, or timid.

110. Fifth, true devotion to Mary is **disinterested**. It inspires us to seek God alone in his Blessed Mother and not ourselves. The true subject of Mary does not serve his illustrious Queen for selfish gain. He does not serve her for temporal or eternal well-being, but simply and solely because she ought to be served and God alone in her.

Daily Prayers to Recite: Litany of the Holy Ghost, Litany of the Blessed Virgin Mary, Ave Maris Stella, St. Louis de Montfort's Prayer to Mary, and the Rosary (see text of prayers at end of text; see Chapter 2 for instructions on reciting the Rosary)

DAY 23

Reading: *True Devotion to the Blessed Virgin Mary*, Nos. 120-121, "Nature of perfect devotion to the Blessed Virgin or perfect consecration to Jesus Christ"

120. All perfection consists in our being conformed, united, and consecrated to Jesus. It naturally follows that the most perfect of all devotions is that which conforms, unites, and consecrates us most completely to Jesus. Of all God's creatures, Mary is the most conformed to Jesus.

Therefore, of all devotions, devotion to Mary makes for the most effective consecration and conformity to Jesus. The more one is consecrated to Mary, the more one is consecrated to Jesus. That is why perfect consecration to Jesus is a perfect and complete consecration of oneself to the Blessed Virgin. This is the devotion I teach. In other words, it is the perfect renewal of the vows and promises of Holy Baptism.

121. This devotion consists in giving oneself entirely to Mary in order to belong entirely to Jesus through her. It requires us to give the following:

(1) Our body with its senses and members;
(2) Our soul with its faculties;
(3) Our present material possessions and all we shall acquire in the future; and
(4) Our interior and spiritual possessions, that is, our merits, virtues, and good actions of the past, the present, and the future.

In other words, we give Mary all that we possess both in our natural life and in our spiritual life. Not only that, we give Mary everything we will acquire in the future in the order of nature, of grace, and of glory in heaven. This we do without the slightest reservation. We don't hold back even a penny, a hair, or the smallest good deed. And we give all this for all eternity without claiming or expecting anything in return for our offering and our service, except the honor of belonging to our Lord through Mary and in Mary. This we would do even if our Mother was not - as in fact she always is - the most generous and appreciative of all God's creatures.

Daily Prayers to Recite: Litany of the Holy Ghost, Litany of the Blessed Virgin Mary, Ave Maris Stella, St. Louis de Montfort's Prayer to Mary, and the Rosary (see text of prayers at end of text; see Chapter 2 for instructions on reciting the Rosary)

DAY 24

Reading: *True Devotion to the Blessed Virgin Mary*, Nos. 152-164

This devotion is a smooth, short, perfect, and sure way of attaining union with our Lord Jesus, in which Christian perfection consists.

This devotion is a **smooth** way. It is the path which Jesus Christ, Himself, opened up in coming to us. Along this path, there is no obstruction to prevent us reaching him. It is quite true that we can attain to divine union by other roads, but these involve many more crosses, exceptional setbacks, and difficulties that we cannot easily overcome.

This devotion is a **short** way to discover Jesus. The road is short because we do not wander from it. The road is also short because, as we have just said, we walk along this road with greater ease and joy, and therefore with greater speed. We advance more in a brief period of submission to Mary and dependence on her than in whole years of self-will and self-reliance.

This devotion is a **perfect** way to reach our Lord and be united to him. This is because Mary is the most perfect and the most holy of all creatures, and because Jesus, who came to us in a perfect manner, chose no other road for his great and wonderful journey. The Most High, the Incomprehensible One, the Inaccessible One, He who is, deigned to come down to us poor earthly creatures who are nothing at all. How was this done? The Most High God came down to us in a perfect way through the humble Virgin Mary, without losing anything of his divinity or holiness. It is likewise through Mary that we poor creatures must ascend to almighty God in a perfect manner and without fear.

This devotion to our Lady is a **sure** way to go to Jesus and to acquire holiness through union with Him. The devotion which I teach is not new. Indeed, it could not be condemned without overthrowing the foundations of Christianity. It is obvious then that this devotion is not new. If it is not commonly practiced, it is because it is too sublime to be appreciated and undertaken by everyone. This devotion is a safe means of going to Jesus Christ, because it is Mary's role to lead us safely to her Son.

Daily Prayers to Recite: Litany of the Holy Ghost, Litany of the Blessed Virgin Mary, Ave Maris Stella, St. Louis de Montfort's Prayer to Mary, and the Rosary (see text of prayers at end of text; see Chapter 2 for instructions on reciting the Rosary)

DAY 25

Reading: *True Devotion to the Blessed Virgin Mary*, Nos. 213-225, "Wonderful Effects of this Devotion"

My dear friend, be sure that if you remain faithful to the interior and exterior practices of this devotion, which I will point out, the following effects will be produced in your soul:

1. Knowledge of our unworthiness
By the light which the Holy Spirit will give you through Mary, his faithful spouse, you will perceive the evil inclinations of your fallen nature and how incapable you are of good. Finally, the humble Virgin Mary will share her humility with you so that, although you regard yourself with distaste and desire to be disregarded by others, you will not look down on anyone.

2. A share in Mary's faith
Mary will share her faith with you. Her faith on earth was stronger than that of all the patriarchs, prophets, apostles, and saints.

3. The gift of pure love
The Mother of fair love will rid your heart of all scruples and inordinate servile fear.

4. Great confidence in God and in Mary
Our Blessed Lady will fill you with unbounded confidence in God and in herself. This is because you will no longer approach Jesus by yourself but always through Mary, your loving Mother.

5. Communication of the spirit of Mary

The soul of Mary will be communicated to you to glorify the Lord. Her spirit will take the place of yours to rejoice in God, her Savior, but only if you are faithful to the practices of this devotion.

6. Transformation into the likeness of Jesus
Mary, the Tree of Life, will be well cultivated in your soul by fidelity to this devotion. She will in due time bring forth her fruit, which is none other than Jesus.

7. The Greater Glory of Christ
If you live this devotion sincerely, you will give more glory to Jesus in a month than in many years of a more demanding devotion.

Daily Prayers to Recite: Litany of the Holy Ghost, Litany of the Blessed Virgin Mary, Ave Maris Stella, St. Louis de Montfort's Prayer to Mary, and the Rosary (see text of prayers at end of text; see Chapter 2 for instructions on reciting the Rosary)

DAY 26

Reading: *True Devotion to the Blessed Virgin Mary*, Nos. 12-38

"If you wish to understand the Mother," says a saint, "then understand the Son. She is a worthy Mother of God." Hic taceat omnis lingua: Here let every tongue be silent. My heart has dictated with special joy all that I have written to show that Mary has been unknown up till now, and that that is one of the reasons why Jesus Christ is not known as he should be. If then, as is certain, the knowledge and the kingdom of Jesus Christ must come into the world, it can only be as a necessary consequence of the knowledge and reign of Mary. She who first gave him to the world will establish his kingdom in the world.

With the whole Church I acknowledge that Mary, being a mere creature fashioned by the hands of God is, compared to his infinite majesty, less than an atom, or rather is simply nothing, since he alone can say, "I am he who is". Consequently, this great Lord, who is ever independent and self-sufficient, never had and does not now have any absolute need of the Blessed Virgin for the accomplishment of his will and the manifestation of his glory. To do all things he has only to will them. However, I declare that, considering things as they are, because God has decided to begin and accomplish his greatest works through the Blessed Virgin ever since he created her, we can safely believe that he will not change his plan in the time to come, for he is God and therefore does not change in his thoughts or his way of acting.

Mary is the Queen of heaven and earth by grace as Jesus is king by nature and by conquest. But as the kingdom of Jesus Christ exists primarily in the heart or interior of man, according to the words of the Gospel, "The kingdom of God is within you", so the kingdom of the Blessed Virgin is principally in the interior of man, that is, in his soul. It is principally in souls that she is glorified with her Son more than in any visible creature. So we may call her, as the saints do, Queen of our hearts.

Daily Prayers to Recite: Litany of the Holy Ghost, Litany of the Blessed Virgin Mary, Ave Maris Stella, St. Louis de Montfort's Prayer to Mary, and the Rosary (see text of prayers at end of text; see Chapter 2 for instructions on reciting the Rosary)

THIRD WEEK

DAY 27

Theme for the Week: Knowledge of Jesus Christ

During this period we will apply ourselves to the study of Jesus Christ. What is to be studied about Christ? First the God-Man, His grace and glory. Then, His rights to sovereign dominion over us; since, after having renounced Satan and the world, we have taken Jesus Christ for our Lord. The next object of our study is Jesus' exterior actions and His interior life. These include the virtues and acts of His Sacred Heart, His association with Mary in the mysteries of the Annunciation and Incarnation, His infancy and hidden life, the feast of Cana, and on Calvary.

Reading: *True Devotion to the Blessed Virgin Mary*, Nos. 61-62

61. Jesus, our Saviour, who is true God and true man, must be the ultimate end of all our devotions; otherwise they would be false and misleading. He is the Alpha and the Omega, the beginning and end of everything. "We labor," says St. Paul, "only to make all men perfect in Jesus Christ." For in Jesus alone dwells the entire fullness of the divinity and the complete fullness of grace, virtue, and perfection. In Jesus alone, we have been blessed with every spiritual blessing. Jesus is the only teacher from whom we must learn. Jesus is the only Lord on whom we should depend. Jesus is the only Head to whom we should be united, and the only model that we should imitate. Jesus is the only Physician that can

162

heal us; the only Shepherd that can feed us; the only Way that can lead us; the only Truth that we can believe; the only Life that can animate us. Jesus alone is everything to us, and He alone can satisfy all our desires. We are given no other name under heaven by which we can be saved. God has laid no other foundation for our salvation, perfection, and glory than Jesus. Every edifice which is not built on that firm rock, is founded upon shifting sands and will certainly fall sooner or later. Through him, with him, and in him, we can do all things and render all honor and glory to the Father in the unity of the Holy Spirit; we can make ourselves perfect; and we can be for our neighbor a fragrance of eternal life.

62. We are establishing sound devotion to our Blessed Mother *only* in order to establish devotion to our Lord more perfectly, by providing a smooth but certain way of reaching Jesus Christ. If devotion to our Lady distracts us from our Lord, we would have to reject it as an illusion of the devil. But this is far from being the case. As I have already shown and will show again later on, this devotion is necessary, simply and solely because it is a way of reaching Jesus perfectly, loving him tenderly, and serving him faithfully.

Daily Prayers to Recite: Litany of the Holy Ghost, Ave Maris Stella, Litany to the Holy Name, St. Louis de Montfort's Prayer to Mary, and O Jesus Living in Mary (see text of prayers at end of text)

DAY 28

Reading: Matthew 26:1-2, 26-29, 36-46

When Jesus had finished all these sayings, he said to his disciples: "You know that after two days the Passover is coming, and the Son of man will be delivered up to be crucified."

Now as they were eating, Jesus took bread, and blessed, and broke it, and gave it to the disciples and said, "Take, eat; this is my body." And he took a cup, and when he had given thanks he gave it to them, saying, "Drink of it, all of you; for this is my blood of the covenant, which is poured out for many for the forgiveness of sins. I tell you I shall not drink again of this fruit of the vine until that day when I drink it new with you in my Father's kingdom."

Then Jesus went with them to a place called Gethsemane, and he said to his disciples, "Sit here, while I go yonder and pray." And taking with him Peter and the two sons of Zebedee, he began to be sorrowful and troubled. Then he said to them, "My soul is very sorrowful, even to death; remain here, and watch with me." And going a little farther he fell on his face and prayed, "My Father, if it be possible, let this cup pass from me; nevertheless, not as I will, but as thou wilt." And he came to the disciples and found them sleeping; and he said to Peter, "So, could you not watch with me one hour? Watch and pray that you may not enter into temptation; the spirit indeed is willing, but the flesh is weak." Again, for the second time, he went away and prayed, "My Father, if this cannot pass unless I drink it, thy will be done." And again he came and found them sleeping, for their eyes were heavy. So, leaving them again, he went away and prayed for the third time, saying the same words. Then he came to the disciples and said to them, "Are you still sleeping and taking your rest? Behold, the hour is at hand, and the Son of man is betrayed into the hands of sinners. Rise, let us be going; see, my betrayer is at hand."

Daily Prayers to Recite: Litany of the Holy Ghost, Ave Maris Stella, Litany to the Holy Name, St. Louis de Montfort's Prayer to Mary, and O Jesus Living in Mary (see text of prayers at end of text)

DAY 29

Reading: *Imitation of Christ* by Thomas á Kempis, Book I, Chapter 1, "Of the Imitation of Christ and Contempt for all the Vanities of the World"

He that follows Me, walks not in darkness (John 8:12), says the Lord. These words of Christ admonish us to imitate His life and manners to be truly enlightened and delivered from all blindness of heart.

Therefore, let our chief endeavor be to meditate upon the life of Jesus Christ. The teachings of Christ exceed all the words of the angels and saints. He whose soul beholds the Gospel will find therein the hidden manna (Revelation 2:17). But oftentimes, many who hear the Gospel of Christ, do not find such sweetness in them. This is because they do not have the Spirit of Christ. But whoever will fully understand the words of Christ, must conform his life wholly to the life of Christ.

What does it avail a man to speak profoundly of the Trinity, if he lacks of humility and thereby displeases the Trinity? Profound words do not make a man holy and just. It is a life of virtue which makes him dear to God. I would rather feel contrition for my sins, than merely know the definition of contrition. If you knew the whole Bible by heart and the writings of all the philosophers, what would it profit you without the love of God and His grace?

Vanity of vanities, all is vanity (Ecclesiastes 1:2), except to love God and to serve Him only. This is the highest wisdom: to draw daily nearer to God and the kingdom of heaven by despising the world.

Daily Prayers to Recite: Litany of the Holy Ghost, Ave Maris Stella, Litany to the Holy Name, St. Louis de Montfort's Prayer to Mary, and O Jesus Living in Mary (see text of prayers at end of text)

DAY 30

Reading 1: Matthew 27:36-44

Then [the soldiers] sat down and kept watch over him there. And over his head they put the charge against him, which read, "This is Jesus the King of the Jews." Then two robbers were crucified with him, one on the right and one on the left. And those who passed by derided him, wagging their heads and saying, "You who would destroy the temple and build it in three days, save yourself! If you are the Son of God, come down from the cross." So also the chief priests, with the scribes and elders, mocked him, saying, "He saved others; he cannot save himself. He is the King of Israel; let him come down now from the cross, and we will believe in him. He trusts in God; let God deliver him now, if he desires him; for he said, 'I am the Son of God.'" And the robbers who were crucified with him also reviled him in the same way.

Reading 2: *Imitation of Christ* by Thomas á Kempis, Book II, Chapter 12, "Of the King's High Way of the Holy Cross"

To many this seems a hard saying, "Deny yourself, take up your cross, and follow Me" (Matt. 16:24). But it will be much harder to hear this at the Last Judgment, "Depart from Me, you cursed, into everlasting fire" (Matt. 25:41). But they who now gladly hear and follow the words of Christ, need not fear hearing a sentence of eternal damnation. This sign of the Cross will appear in heaven when the Lord comes to judge the world (Matt. 24:30). Then all the servants of the Cross, who in their lifetime conformed themselves to Christ crucified, shall draw near to Christ the Judge with great confidence.

Why, then, do you fear to take up His Cross? It is the one and only way which leads to Heaven. In the Cross is salvation, in the Cross is life, in the Cross is protection against our enemies, in the Cross is the fullness of heavenly sweetness. In the Cross is strength of mind, in the Cross is joy of spirit, in the Cross is the height of virtue, in the Cross is the perfection of holiness.

Take up, therefore, your Cross and follow Jesus into life everlasting.

Daily Prayers to Recite: Litany of the Holy Ghost, Ave Maris Stella, Litany to the Holy Name, St. Louis de Montfort's Prayer to Mary, and O Jesus Living in Mary (see text of prayers at end of text)

Day 31

Reading 1: *Imitation of Christ* by Thomas á Kempis, Book IV, Chapter 2, "That the Great Goodness of God is Given to Man in the Blessed Sacrament"

My Lord Jesus, confident of your goodness and great mercy, I draw near. I come to You as a sick man comes to the Healer, as a hungry and thirsty man comes to the Fountain of life, as a needy man to the King of Heaven. I come as a servant to the Lord, a creature to the Creator, and as afflicted to the Comforter.

"But how is it that You come to me? Who am I that You give Yourself to me? How dare I, a sinner, appear before You? And how is it that You would come to such a sinner? You know me and are well aware that I have nothing to repay You with for such grace. I confess, therefore, my own unworthiness and acknowledge Your goodness. I praise Your tender mercy and give thanks for your infinite charity.

Reading 2: *True Devotion to the Blessed Virgin Mary*, Nos. 243-254

Loving slaves of Jesus in Mary should hold in high esteem the devotion to Jesus, the Word of God, in the great mystery of the Incarnation, March 25th (Feast of the Annunciation). This is the mystery proper to this devotion, because it was inspired by the Holy Spirit for the following reasons:

- That we might honor and imitate the wondrous dependence which God the Son chose to have on Mary, for the glory of His Father and for the redemption of man. This dependence is revealed especially in this mystery where Jesus becomes a captive and slave in

168

the womb of his Blessed Mother, depending on her for everything.

- That we might thank God for the incomparable graces he has conferred upon Mary, especially that of choosing her to be his most worthy Mother. This choice was made in the mystery of the Incarnation. These are the two principal ends of the slavery of Jesus in Mary.

We live in an age of pride when a great number of haughty scholars find fault even with long-established and sound devotions. Because of these, it is better to speak of "slavery of Jesus in Mary" and to call oneself "slave of Jesus" rather than "slave of Mary". We then avoid giving any pretext for criticism. In this way, we name this devotion after its ultimate end which is Jesus, rather than after the way and the means to arrive there, which is Mary. However, we can very well use either term without any scruple, as I myself do.

The principal mystery celebrated and honored in this devotion is the mystery of the Incarnation when we find Jesus only in Mary, having become incarnate in her womb. Therefore, it is appropriate for us to say, "slavery of Jesus in Mary," and of Jesus dwelling enthroned in Mary, "O Jesus living in Mary," according to the beautiful prayer recited by so many great souls.

Those who accept this devotion should have a great love for the "Hail Mary", or, as it is also called, the "Angelic Salutation". Few Christians, however enlightened they may be, understand the value, merit, excellence, and necessity of the Hail Mary. Our Blessed Lady herself had to appear on several occasions to men of great holiness and insight, such as St. Dominic, St. John Capistrano, and Blessed Alan de Rupe, to convince them of the richness of this prayer.

Daily Prayers to Recite: Litany of the Holy Ghost, Ave Maris Stella, Litany to the Holy Name, St. Louis de Montfort's Prayer to Mary, and O Jesus Living in Mary (see text of prayers at end of text)

DAY 32

Reading 1: *Imitation of Christ* by Thomas á Kempis, Book II, Chapter 7, "Of the Love of Jesus above All Things"

Blessed is he who knows how good it is to love Jesus and to despise himself for Jesus' sake. A man ought to forsake what he loves for the sake of the Beloved, because Jesus must be loved above all things (Deut. 6:5; Matt. 22:37).

The love of created things is deceitful and disappointing, while the love of Jesus is faithful and persevering. He who clings to a creature will fall as that creature falls, while he who embraces Jesus will be made strong forever.

Love Jesus and hold onto Him as your friend. When all others forsake you, He will not. Nor will Jesus allow you to perish in the end. At some point whether you choose to or not, you will be separated from all men. Therefore, both in life and death, keep yourself close to Jesus. Commit yourself to faithfulness to Him, Who remains and will help you even when all else fail.

Your Beloved is of such a nature, that He will allow no rival. Jesus alone will have your heart, which is His throne, and He will rule there as King. If you could empty yourself completely of the love of creatures, Jesus would dwell with you and never forsake you.

Reading 2: *True Devotion to the Blessed Virgin Mary,* Nos. 61-62

There are some interior practices which are very sanctifying for those souls which the Holy Spirit calls to a high degree of perfection. They may be expressed in four words: doing everything *through* Mary, *with* Mary, *in* Mary, and *for* Mary. We do these that we may do it more perfectly *through* Jesus, *with* Jesus, *in* Jesus, and *for* Jesus.

Through Mary
We must do everything through Mary. That is, we must obey her always and be led in all things by her spirit, which is the Holy Spirit of God. "Those who are led by the Spirit of God are children of God," says St. Paul. Those who are led by the spirit of Mary are children of Mary, and, therefore, children of God.

Among the many servants of Mary only those who are truly and faithfully devoted to her are led by her spirit. I have said that the spirit of Mary is the Spirit of God because she was never led by her own spirit, but always by the Holy Spirit. The Holy Spirit made Himself master of her to such an extent that He became her very spirit. That is why St. Ambrose says, "May the soul of Mary be in each one of us to glorify the Lord. May the spirit of Mary be in each one of us to rejoice in God."

Happy is the man who follows the example of the good Jesuit Brother Rodriguez. Rodriguez died a holy death, because he was completely possessed and governed by the spirit of

Mary, a spirit which is gentle yet strong, zealous yet prudent, humble yet courageous, pure yet fruitful.

With Mary
We must do everything with Mary. That is to say, we must look upon Mary in all our actions. Although she was a simple human being, she is the perfect model of every virtue and perfection. She was fashioned by the Holy Spirit for us to imitate, as far as our limited capacity allows.

In every action, we should consider how Mary performed it or how she would perform it if she were in our place. For this reason, we must examine and meditate on the great virtues she practiced during her life, especially:

1. Her lively faith, by which she believed the angel's word without the least hesitation, and believed faithfully and constantly even to the foot of the Cross on Calvary; and
2. Her deep humility, which made her prefer seclusion, maintain silence, submit to every eventuality, and put herself in the last place.

Daily Prayers to Recite: Litany of the Holy Ghost, Ave Maris Stella, Litany to the Holy Name, St. Louis de Montfort's Prayer to Mary, and O Jesus Living in Mary (see text of prayers at end of text)

DAY 33

Reading 1: *Imitation of Christ* by Thomas á Kempis, Book IV, Chapter 11, "That the Body and Blood of Christ and Holy Scripture are Most Necessary for the Health of a Man's Soul"

Lord Jesus, how sweet it is to the devout soul to feast with You in Your banquet, where there is no other food but Yourself, which is the only Beloved of the devout soul and most desired in his heart! To me, it would also be sweet to pour forth tears in Your Presence from the very bottom of my heart. Sweeter still, would it be to wash Your feet with my tears alongside the blessed woman, Mary Magdalene (Luke 7:38).

But where is that devotion? Where is that bountiful flowing of holy tears? Surely in the sight of You and Your holy Angels, my whole heart ought to burn and to weep for joy. For in this Sacrament, You are mystically present and hidden under another shape.

And why? My eyes would not be able to endure looking upon You in Your Divine brightness. Neither could even the whole world stand in the glorious splendor of Your majesty. In this, You have regard for my weakness, that You would hide Yourself under this Sacrament.

Reading 2: *True Devotion to the Blessed Virgin Mary*, Nos. 261-65

As we discussed yesterday, there are some interior practices which are very sanctifying. They may be expressed in four words: doing everything *through* Mary, *with* Mary, *in* Mary, and *for* Mary. We discussed *through* and *with* Mary yesterday, and will turn now to *in* and *for* Mary. Remember, we do these that we may do it more perfectly *through* Jesus, *with* Jesus, *in* Jesus, and *for* Jesus.

In Mary

We must do everything in Mary. To understand this, we must realize that the Blessed Virgin is the true **Eden**. She is the earthly paradise of the new Adam, and the ancient paradise was only a symbol pointing toward her. There are in this earthly paradise untold riches, beauties, rarities, and delights. These were all left there by the new Adam, Jesus Christ. It is in this paradise that for nine months He "took his delights", worked his wonders, and displayed his riches with the magnificence of God, Himself.

The real **Tree of Life** grows in this earthly paradise. This is the Tree of Life which bore our Lord, who is the Fruit of Life. This is also the real Tree of Knowledge of Good and Evil, which bore the Light of the world. In this divine place, there are trees planted by the hand of God and watered by His divine unction. These trees have borne and continue to bear fruit that is pleasing to Him.

Only the Holy Spirit can teach us the truths that these material objects symbolize. The Holy Spirit, speaking through the Fathers of the Church, calls Our Lady the **Eastern Gate**. It is through the Eastern Gate that the High Priest, Jesus Christ, enters and goes out into the world. Through this gate He entered the world the first time, and through this same gate He will come the second time.

For Mary
Finally, we must do everything for Mary. We take Mary for our proximate, not ultimate, end. She is our mysterious intermediary and the easiest way of reaching Him. Relying on her protection, we should undertake and carry out great things for our noble Queen. We must defend her privileges when they are questioned and uphold her good name when it is under attack. We must attract everyone, if possible, to

her service and to this true and sound devotion. As a reward for these little services, we should expect nothing in return, save the honor of belonging to such a lovable Queen and the joy of being united through her to Jesus, her Son, by a bond that is indissoluble in time and in eternity.

Daily Prayers to Recite: Litany of the Holy Ghost, Ave Maris Stella, Litany to the Holy Name, St. Louis de Montfort's Prayer to Mary, and O Jesus Living in Mary (see text of prayers at end of text)

DAY 34: DAY OF CONSECRATION

On the Day of Consecration, either fast, give alms, or offer a votive candle for the good of another (or all of the above). Do some spiritual penance and approach consecration in the spirit of mortification.

Now, go to Confession. If it is not possible to go to Confession on the Day of Consecration, go during the eight days prior.

Having gone to Confession, next receive Communion with the intention of giving yourself to Jesus, as a slave of love, by the hands of Mary. Try to receive Communion according to the method described in the Supplement of the book, "True Devotion to the Blessed Virgin Mary." See "Method of Communion" supplement below.

Now, pray the words of the consecration. Bring a copy of this consecration, such as the one provided in *The Catholic ManBook*, with you to church. Read it after Mass, either in front of the tabernacle or before the exposed Blessed Sacrament would be ideal. Sign your copy of the Act of Consecration.

Here are the words of consecration:

O, Eternal and Incarnate Wisdom! O sweetest and most adorable Jesus! True God and true man, only Son of the Eternal Father, and of Mary, always virgin! I adore You profoundly in the bosom and splendors of Your Father during eternity, and I adore You also in the virginal bosom of Mary, Your most worthy Mother, in the time of Your incarnation.

I give You thanks that You have annihilated Yourself, taking the form of a slave in order to rescue me from the cruel slavery of the devil. I praise and glorify You for You have been pleased to submit Yourself to Mary, Your holy Mother, in all things, in order to make me Your faithful slave through her.

But, alas! Ungrateful and faithless as I have been, I have not kept the promises which I made so solemnly to You in my Baptism. I have not fulfilled my obligations. I do not deserve to be called Your child, nor even Your slave. As there is nothing in me which does not merit Your anger and repulse, I dare not come by myself before You, most holy and august Majesty. It is on this account that I have recourse to the intercession of Your most holy Mother, whom You have given me for a mediatrix with You. It is through her that I hope to obtain from You the following: contrition, the pardon of my sins, and the acquisition and preservation of wisdom.

Hail, then, O Immaculate Mary, living tabernacle of the Divinity, where the Eternal Wisdom willed to be hidden and to be adored by angels and by men! Hail, O Queen of Heaven and earth, to whose empire everything is subject which is under God. Hail, O sure refuge of sinners, whose mercy fails no one. Hear the desires which I have of the Divine Wisdom. For that end, receive the vows and offerings which I present to you in my lowliness.

I, _____ *[your name]*, a faithless sinner, renew and ratify today in your hands the vows of my Baptism. I renounce forever Satan, his pomps and works. I give myself entirely to Jesus Christ, the Incarnate Wisdom, to carry my cross after Him all the days of my life, and to be more faithful to Him than I have ever been before. In the presence of all the heavenly court, I choose you this day for my Mother and Mistress. I deliver and consecrate to you, as your slave, my body and soul, my goods, both interior and exterior, and even the value of all my good actions, past, present, and future. I leave to you the entire and full right of disposing of me and all that belongs to me, without exception, according to your good pleasure, for the greater glory of God in time and in eternity.

Receive, O kindest Virgin, this little offering of my slavery, in honor of, and in union with, that subjection which the Eternal Wisdom deigned to have to your maternity. Receive this little offering in homage to the power which both of you have over this poor sinner. Receive this little offering also in thanksgiving for the privileges with which the Holy Trinity has favored you. I declare that I wish henceforth, as your true slave, to seek your honor and to obey you in all things.

O admirable Mother, present me to your dear Son as His eternal slave. As He has redeemed me by you, by you may He receive me! O Mother of mercy, grant me the grace to obtain the true Wisdom of God. For that end, receive me among those whom you love and teach, whom you lead, nourish, and protect as your children and your slaves.

O faithful Virgin, make me in all things so perfect a disciple, imitator, and slave of the Incarnate Wisdom, Jesus Christ thy Son, that I may attain, by your intercession and by your example, to the fullness of His age on earth and of His glory in Heaven. Amen.

_____

Sign your name here

_____

Date

AFTER CONSECRATION

Once you have consecrated yourself to Jesus through Mary, *live* that consecration. St. Louis-Marie de Montfort, the author of this Marian consecration, recommended the following:

- Keep praying to develop a "great contempt" for the spirit of this world and material things.
- Maintain a special devotion to the Mystery of the Incarnation. This can be done through meditation, spiritual reading, or by focusing on the feasts centering around the Incarnation, such as the Annunciation and the Nativity.
- Frequently recite the Hail Mary, Rosary, and the Magnificat. You may have discovered new Marian

prayers during this consecration, such as the "Ave Maris Stella" or one of the litanies, that you may want to begin reciting, as well.

- Recite, every day if it is not inconvenient, the "Little Crown of the Blessed Virgin". This is a series of Our Fathers, Hail Marys, and Glory Bes, one Hail Mary for each of the twelve stars in the Virgin's Crown. St. Louis has a special way of praying the Little Crown, which is recommended.

- Do everything through, with, in, and for Mary for the sake of Jesus, with the prayer, "I am all thine Immaculate One, with all that I have in time and in eternity" in your heart and on your lips.

- Associate yourself with Mary in a special way before, during, and after Communion. See "Method of Communion" supplement below.

- Wear a little iron chain, such as around the neck, arm, waist, or ankle, as an outward sign and reminder of your holy slavery. This practice is optional, but very recommended by St. Louis, though he does not further specify the appearance of such a chain.

- Renew the consecration once a year on the same date as signed above or another Feast day of your choosing, and by following the same 33-day period of exercises. If desired, also renew the consecration monthly with the prayer, "I am all yours and all I have is yours, O dear Jesus, through Mary, Your holy Mother."

- Join a Confraternity of Mary, such the Confraternity of Mary, Queen of All Hearts.

SUPPLEMENT:
THIS DEVOTION AT
HOLY COMMUNION

[From *True Devotion to Mary*, Nos. 266-273]

Before Holy Communion

1. Place yourself humbly in the presence of God.
2. Renounce your corrupt nature and dispositions, no matter how good self-love makes them appear to you.
3. Renew your consecration saying, "I belong entirely to you, dear Mother, and all that I have is yours."
4. Implore Mary to lend you her heart so that you may receive her Son with her dispositions. Remind her that her Son's glory requires that He should not come into a heart so sullied and fickle as your own, which could not fail to diminish His glory and might cause Him to leave. Tell her that if she will take up her home in you to receive her Son - which she can do because of her sovereignty over all hearts - He will be received by her in a perfect manner without danger

of being affronted or being forced to depart. "God is in the midst of her. She shall not be moved."

5. Tell her with confidence that all you have given her of your possessions is little enough to honor her, but that in Holy Communion you wish to give her the same gifts as the eternal Father gave her. She will feel more honored than if you gave her all the wealth in the world.

6. Tell her, finally, that Jesus, whose love for her is unique, still wishes to take His delight and His repose in her even in your soul. And this, even though your soul is poorer and less clean than the stable which He readily entered, because she was there. Beg her to lend you her heart, saying, "O Mary, I take you for my all. Give me your heart."

During Holy Communion

After the Our Father, when you are about to receive our Lord, say to Him three times the prayer, "Lord, I am not worthy," as you would say it to each member of the Trinity:

1. Say it the first time as if you were telling the eternal Father that because of your evil thoughts and your ingratitude to such a good Father, you are unworthy to receive his only-begotten Son. But here is Mary, His handmaid, who acts for you and whose presence gives you a special confidence and hope in Him.

2. Say to God the Son, "Lord, I am not worthy." Say it meaning that you are not worthy to receive Him because of your useless and evil words and your carelessness in His service. Nevertheless, you ask Him to have pity on you because you are going to usher Him into the house of His Mother and yours, and you will not let Him go until He has made it His home. Implore Him to rise and come to the place of His repose and the ark of His sanctification. Tell Him that you

have no faith in your own merits, strength, and preparedness, like Esau, but only in Mary, your Mother, just as Jacob had trust in Rebecca his mother. Tell Him that although you are a great sinner, you still presume to approach Him, supported by His holy Mother and adorned with her merits and virtues.

3. Say to the Holy Spirit, "Lord, I am not worthy". Tell Him that you are not worthy to receive the masterpiece of His love because of your lukewarmness, wickedness, and resistance to His inspirations. But, nonetheless, you put all your confidence in Mary, His faithful Spouse, and say with St. Bernard, "She is my greatest safeguard, the whole foundation of my hope." Beg Him to overshadow Mary, His inseparable Spouse, once again. Her womb is as pure and her heart as ardent as ever. Tell Him that if He does not enter your soul neither Jesus nor Mary will be formed there, nor will it be a worthy dwelling for them.

After Holy Communion

After Holy Communion, close your eyes and recollect yourself. Then usher Jesus into the heart of Mary. You are giving Him to His Mother. She will receive Him with great love, give Him the place of honor, adore Him profoundly, show Him perfect love, embrace Him intimately in spirit and in truth, and perform many offices for Him of which we, in our ignorance, would know nothing.

Or, maintain a profoundly humble heart in the presence of Jesus dwelling in Mary. Be in attendance like a slave at the gate of the royal palace, where the King is speaking with the Queen. While they are talking to each other, with no need of you, go in spirit to heaven and to the whole world. Call then upon all creatures to thank, adore, and love Jesus and Mary for you. "Come, let us adore."

Or, ask Jesus living in Mary that His kingdom may come upon earth through His holy Mother. Ask for divine wisdom, divine love, the forgiveness of your sins, or any other grace, but always through Mary and in Mary. Cast a look of reproach upon yourself and say, "Lord, do not look at my sins, let Your eyes see nothing in me, but the virtues and merits of Mary."

Remembering your sins, you may add, "I am my own worst enemy, and I am guilty of all these sins." Or, "Deliver me from the unjust and deceitful man that I am." Or again, "Dear Jesus, you must increase in my soul and I must decrease." "Mary, you must increase in me and I must always go on decreasing." "O Jesus and Mary, increase in me and increase in others around me."

There are innumerable other thoughts with which the Holy Spirit will inspire you, which He will make yours if you are thoroughly recollected and mortified, and constantly faithful to the great and sublime devotion which I have been teaching you.

But remember, the more you let Mary act in your communion, the more Jesus will be glorified. The more you humble yourself and listen to Jesus and Mary in peace and silence - with no desire to see, taste, or feel - the more freedom you will give to Mary to act in Jesus' name and the more Jesus will act in Mary. For the just man lives everywhere by faith, but especially in Holy Communion, which is an act of faith.

Appendix:
Prayers Recited
during the Con-
secration

Veni Creator

Come, Holy Spirit, Creator blest,
and in our souls take up Thy rest;
come with Thy grace and heavenly aid
to fill the hearts which Thou hast made.

O comforter, to Thee we cry,
O heavenly gift of God Most High,
O fount of life and fire of love,
and sweet anointing from above.

Thou in Thy sevenfold gifts are known;
Thou, finger of God's hand we own;
Thou, promise of the Father,
Thou Who dost the tongue with power imbue.

Kindle our sense from above,
and make our hearts o'erflow with love;
with patience firm and virtue high
the weakness of our flesh supply.

Far from us drive the foe we dread,
and grant us Thy peace instead;
so shall we not, with Thee for guide,
turn from the path of life aside.

Oh, may Thy grace on us bestow
the Father and the Son to know;
and Thee, through endless times confessed,
of both the eternal Spirit blest.

Now to the Father and the Son,
Who rose from death, be glory given,
with Thou, O Holy Comforter,
henceforth by all in earth and heaven. Amen.

AVE MARIS STELLA

Hail, O Star of the ocean,
God's own Mother blest,
ever sinless Virgin,
gate of heav'nly rest.

Taking that sweet Ave,
which from Gabriel came,
peace confirm within us,
changing Eve's name.

Break the sinners' fetters,
make our blindness day,
Chase all evils from us,

for all blessings pray.

Show thyself a Mother,
may the Word divine
born for us thine Infant
hear our prayers through thine.

Virgin all excelling,
mildest of the mild,
free from guilt preserve us
meek and undefiled.

Keep our life all spotless,
make our way secure
till we find in Jesus,
joy for evermore.

Praise to God the Father,
honor to the Son,
in the Holy Spirit,
be the glory one. Amen

MAGNIFICAT
(Lk 1:46-55)

My soul proclaims the greatness of the Lord,
my spirit rejoices in God my Savior
for he has looked with favor on his lowly servant.
From this day all generations will call me blessed:
the Almighty has done great things for me,
and holy is his Name.

He has mercy on those who fear him
in every generation.
He has shown the strength of his arm,
he has scattered the proud in their conceit.

He has cast down the mighty from their thrones,
and has lifted up the lowly.
He has filled the hungry with good things,
and the rich he has sent away empty.

He has come to the help of his servant Israel
for he remembered his promise of mercy,
the promise he made to our fathers,
to Abraham and his children forever. Amen.

GLORY BE
Glory be to the Father,
and to the Son,
and to the Holy Ghost.
As it was in the beginning,
is now,
and ever shall be,
world without end. Amen.

LITANY OF THE HOLY GHOST

Lord, *have mercy on us.*
Christ, *have mercy on us.*
Lord, *have mercy on us.*

Father all powerful, *have mercy on us*
Jesus, Eternal Son of the Father, Redeemer of the world,
save us.
Spirit of the Father and the Son, boundless life of both,
sanctify us.
Holy Trinity, *hear us.*

Holy Ghost, Who proceeds from the Father and the Son,
enter our hearts.
Holy Ghost, Who are equal to the Father and the Son,
enter our hearts.

Promise of God the Father, *have mercy on us.*
Ray of heavenly light, *have mercy on us.*
Author of all good, *have mercy on us.*
Source of heavenly water, *have mercy on us.*
Consuming fire, *have mercy on us.*
Ardent charity, *have mercy on us.*
Spiritual unction, *have mercy on us.*
Spirit of love and truth, *have mercy on us.*
Spirit of wisdom and understanding, *have mercy on us.*
Spirit of counsel and fortitude, *have mercy on us.*
Spirit of knowledge and piety, *have mercy on us.*
Spirit of the fear of the Lord, *have mercy on us.*
Spirit of grace and prayer, *have mercy on us.*
Spirit of peace and meekness, *have mercy on us.*
Spirit of modesty and innocence, *have mercy on us.*
Holy Ghost, the Comforter, *have mercy on us.*

Holy Ghost, the Sanctifier, *have mercy on us.*
Holy Ghost, Who governs the Church, *have mercy on us.*
Gift of God, the Most High, *have mercy on us.*
Spirit Who fills the universe, *have mercy on us.*
Spirit of the adoption of the children of God, *have mercy on us.*

Holy Ghost, inspire us with horror of sin.
Holy Ghost, come and renew the face of the earth.
Holy Ghost, shed Thy light in our souls.
Holy Ghost, engrave Thy law in our hearts
Holy Ghost, inflame us with the flame of Thy love.
Holy Ghost, open to us the treasures of Thy graces
Holy Ghost, teach us to pray well.
Holy Ghost, enlighten us with Thy heavenly inspirations.
Holy Ghost, lead us in the way of salvation
Holy Ghost, grant us the only necessary knowledge.
Holy Ghost, inspire in us the practice of good.
Holy Ghost, grant us the merits of all virtues.
Holy Ghost, make us persevere in justice.
Holy Ghost, be Thou our everlasting reward.

Lamb of God, Who takes away the sins of the world,
Send us Thy Holy Ghost.
Lamb of God, Who takes away the sins of the world,
Pour down into our souls the gifts of the Holy Ghost.
Lamb of God, Who takes away the sins of the world,
Grant us the Spirit of wisdom and piety.

V. Come, Holy Ghost! Fill the hearts of Thy faithful,
R. And enkindle in them the fire of Thy love.

Let Us Pray:

THE CATHOLIC MANBOOK

Grant, o merciful Father, that Your Divine Spirit may enlighten, inflame and purify us, that He may penetrate us with His heavenly dew and make us fruitful in good works, through Our Lord Jesus Christ, Your Son, Who with You, in the unity of the same Spirit, lives and reigns forever and ever. Amen.

LITANY OF THE BLESSED VIRGIN MARY (LITANY OF LORETO)

Lord, *have mercy on us.*
Christ, *have mercy on us.*

Lord, *have mercy on us.*
Christ hear us. *Christ, graciously hear us.*

God, the Father of heaven, *Have mercy on us.*
God, the Son, Redeemer of the world, *Have mercy on us.*
God, the Holy Ghost, *Have mercy on us.*
Holy Trinity, One God, *Have mercy on us.*

Holy Mary, *pray for us.*
Holy Mother of God, *pray for us.*
Holy Virgin of virgins, *pray for us.*
Mother of Christ, *pray for us.*
Mother of divine grace, *pray for us.*
Mother most pure, *pray for us.*
Mother most chaste, *pray for us.*
Mother inviolate, *pray for us.*
Mother undefiled, *pray for us.*
Mother most amiable, *pray for us.*
Mother most admirable, *pray for us.*
Mother of good counsel, *pray for us.*
Mother of our Creator, *pray for us.*
Mother of our Savior, *pray for us.*

Virgin most prudent, *pray for us.*
Virgin most venerable, *pray for us.*
Virgin most renowned, *pray for us.*
Virgin most powerful, *pray for us.*
Virgin most merciful, *pray for us.*
Virgin most faithful, *pray for us.*
Mirror of justice, *pray for us.*
Seat of wisdom, *pray for us.*
Cause of our joy, *pray for us.*
Spiritual vessel, *pray for us.*
Vessel of honor, *pray for us.*
Singular vessel of devotion, *pray for us.*
Mystical rose, *pray for us.*
Tower of David, *pray for us.*
Tower of ivory, *pray for us.*
House of gold, *pray for us.*
Ark of the covenant, *pray for us.*
Gate of Heaven, *pray for us.*
Morning star, *pray for us.*
Health of the sick, *pray for us.*
Refuge of sinners, *pray for us.*
Comforter of the afflicted, *pray for us.*
Help of Christians, *pray for us.*
Queen of angels, *pray for us.*
Queen of patriarchs, *pray for us.*
Queen of prophets, *pray for us.*
Queen of apostles, *pray for us.*
Queen of martyrs, *pray for us.*
Queen of confessors, *pray for us.*
Queen of virgins, *pray for us.*
Queen of all saints, *pray for us.*
Queen conceived without original sin, *pray for us.*
Queen assumed into heaven, *pray for us.*
Queen of the most holy Rosary, *pray for us.*

Queen of peace, *pray for us.*

Lamb of God, who takest away the sins of the world,
Spare us, O Lord.
Lamb of God, who takest away the sins of the world,
Graciously hear us O Lord.
Lamb of God, who takest away the sins of the world,
Have mercy on us.

V. Pray for us, O holy Mother of God.
R. That we may be made worthy of the promises of Christ.

Let us pray:
Grant, O Lord God, we beseech Thee, that we Thy servants may rejoice in continual health of mind and body; and, through the glorious intercession of Blessed Mary ever Virgin, may be freed from present sorrow, and enjoy eternal gladness. Through Christ our Lord. Amen.

LITANY OF THE HOLY NAME OF JESUS

Lord, *have mercy on us.*
Christ, *have mercy on us.*

Lord, *have mercy on us.*
Christ hear us. *Christ, graciously hear us.*

God, the Father of heaven, *Have mercy on us.*
God, the Son, Redeemer of the world, *Have mercy on us.*
God, the Holy Ghost, *Have mercy on us.*
Holy Trinity, One God, *Have mercy on us.*

Jesus, Son of the living God, *have mercy on us.*
Jesus, splendor of the Father, *have mercy on us.*

Jesus, brightness of eternal light, *have mercy on us.*
Jesus, King of glory, *have mercy on us.*
Jesus, sun of justice, *have mercy on us.*
Jesus, Son of the Virgin Mary, *have mercy on us.*
Jesus, most amiable, *have mercy on us.*
Jesus, most admirable, *have mercy on us.*
Jesus, mighty God, *have mercy on us.*
Jesus, Father of the world to come, *have mercy on us.*
Jesus, angel of great counsel, *have mercy on us.*
Jesus, most powerful, *have mercy on us.*
Jesus, most patient, *have mercy on us.*
Jesus, most obedient, *have mercy on us.*
Jesus, meek and humble, *have mercy on us.*
Jesus, lover of chastity, *have mercy on us.*
Jesus, lover of us, *have mercy on us.*
Jesus, God of peace, *have mercy on us.*
Jesus, author of life, *have mercy on us.*
Jesus, model of virtues, *have mercy on us.*
Jesus, lover of souls, *have mercy on us.*
Jesus, our God, *have mercy on us.*
Jesus, our refuge, *have mercy on us.*
Jesus, Father of the poor, *have mercy on us.*
Jesus, treasure of the faithful, *have mercy on us.*
Jesus, Good Shepherd, *have mercy on us.*
Jesus, true light, *have mercy on us.*
Jesus, eternal wisdom, *have mercy on us.*
Jesus, infinite goodness, *have mercy on us.*
Jesus, our way and our life, *have mercy on us.*
Jesus, joy of angels, *have mercy on us.*
Jesus, King of patriarchs, *have mercy on us.*
Jesus, master of Apostles, *have mercy on us.*
Jesus, teacher of Evangelists, *have mercy on us.*
Jesus, strength of martyrs, *have mercy on us.*
Jesus, light of confessors, *have mercy on us.*

Jesus, purity of virgins, *have mercy on us.*
Jesus, crown of all saints, *have mercy on us.*

Be merciful, *spare us, O Jesus.*
Be merciful, *graciously hear us, O Jesus.*

From all evil, *Jesus, deliver us.*
From all sin, *Jesus, deliver us.*
From Thy wrath, *Jesus, deliver us.*
From the snares of the devil, *Jesus, deliver us.*
From the spirit of fornication, *Jesus, deliver us.*
From everlasting death, *Jesus, deliver us.*
From the neglect of Thine inspirations, *Jesus, deliver us.*

Through the mystery of Thy holy Incarnation,
Jesus, deliver us.
Through Thy nativity, *Jesus, deliver us.*
Through Thine infancy, *Jesus, deliver us.*
Through Thy most divine life, *Jesus, deliver us.*
Through Thy labors, *Jesus, deliver us.*
Through Thine agony and Passion, *Jesus, deliver us.*
Through Thy cross and dereliction, *Jesus, deliver us.*
Through Thy sufferings, *Jesus, deliver us.*
Through Thy death and burial, *Jesus, deliver us.*
Through Thy Resurrection, *Jesus, deliver us.*
Through Thine Ascension, *Jesus, deliver us.*
Through Thine institution of the most Holy Eucharist,
Jesus, deliver us.
Through Thy joys, *Jesus, deliver us.*
Through Thy glory, *Jesus, deliver us.*

Lamb of God, Who takest away the sins of the world,
Spare us, O Jesus.
Lamb of God, Who takest away the sins of the world,

Graciously hear us, O Jesus.
Lamb of God, Who takest away the sins of the world,
Have mercy on us.

Jesus, hear us, *Jesus, graciously hear us.*

Let Us Pray. O Lord Jesus Christ, Who hast said: Ask and ye shall receive, seek and ye shall find, knock and it shall be opened unto you; grant, we beseech Thee, to us who ask the gift of Thy divine love, that we may ever love Thee with all our hearts, and in all our words and actions, and never cease from praising Thee.

Give us, O Lord, a perpetual fear and love of Thy holy Name; for Thou never failest to govern those whom Thou dost solidly establish in Thy love, Who livest and reignest world without end. R. Amen.

St. Louis de Montfort's Prayer to Mary

Hail Mary, beloved Daughter of the Eternal Father! Hail Mary, admirable Mother of the Son! Hail Mary, faithful spouse of the Holy Ghost! Hail Mary, my dear Mother, my loving Mistress, my powerful sovereign! Hail my joy, my glory, my heart and my soul! You are all mine by mercy, and I am all yours by justice. But I am not yet sufficiently yours. I now give myself wholly to you without keeping anything back for myself or others. If you still see in me anything which does not belong to you, I beg you to take it and to make yourself the absolute Mistress of all that is mine. Destroy in me all that may be displeasing to God, root it up and bring it to nothing; place and cultivate in me everything that is pleasing to you.

May the light of your faith dispel the darkness of my mind; may your profound humility take the place of my pride; may your sublime contemplation check the distractions of my wandering imagination; may your continuous sight of God fill my memory with His presence; may the burning love of your heart inflame the lukewarmness of mine; may your virtues take the place of my sins; may your merits be my only adornment in the sight of God and make up for all that is wanting in me. Finally, dearly beloved Mother, grant, if it be possible, that I may have no other spirit but yours to know Jesus and His divine will; that I may have no other soul but yours to praise and glorify the Lord; that I may have no other heart but yours to love God with a love as pure and ardent as yours.

I do not ask you for visions, revelations, sensible devotion or spiritual pleasures. It is your privilege to see God clearly. It is your privilege to enjoy heavenly bliss. It is your privilege to triumph gloriously in Heaven at the right hand of your Son and to hold absolute sway over angels, men and demons. It is your privilege to dispose of all the gifts of God, just as you will.

Such is, O heavenly Mary, the "best part," which the Lord has given you and which shall never be taken away from you, and this thought fills my heart with joy. As for my part here below, I wish for nothing more than that which was yours: to believe sincerely without spiritual pleasures; to suffer joyfully without human consolation; to die continually to myself without respite; and to work zealously and unselfishly for you until death as the humblest of your servants.

The only grace I beg you to obtain for me is that every day and every moment of my life I may say: Amen, so be it, to all that you did while on earth; Amen, so be it, to all you are now doing in Heaven; Amen, so be it, to all that you are doing in my soul, so that you alone may fully glorify Jesus in me for time and eternity. Amen.

O JESUS LIVING IN MARY

O Jesus living in Mary,
Come and live in Thy servants,
In the spirit of Thy holiness,
In the fullness of Thy might,
In the truth of Thy virtues,
In the perfection of Thy ways,
In the communion of Thy mysteries;
Subdue every hostile power
In Thy spirit, for the glory of the Father. Amen.

XI.
THANK YOU TO
OUR SPONSORS

MAXIMILLIAN KOLBE
GOLD LEVEL

Associated Food Stores

CHAMPIONS OF MARY
SILVER LEVEL

MICHAEL E. OLINDE, AIF, PPC
Principal
4970 Bluebonnet Blvd., Suite B, Baton Rouge, LA
70809
ph. 225.215.1010   **fx**. 225.928.4466

Paradisus Dei®

Magnificat

HOLY FAMILY
BRONZE LEVEL

A Gladden Sales, LLC Company

Visit at brownpelicanla.com